Henri Lacordaire

Jesus Christ

Conferences delivered at Nôtre Dame in Paris

Henri Lacordaire

Jesus Christ
Conferences delivered at Nôtre Dame in Paris

ISBN/EAN: 9783337429218

Printed in Europe, USA, Canada, Australia, Japan

Cover: Foto ©Lupo / pixelio.de

More available books at **www.hansebooks.com**

JESUS CHRIST:

CONFERENCES

DELIVERED AT

NÔTRE DAME IN PARIS.

BY THE

REV. PÈRE LACORDAIRE,
OF THE ORDER OF SAINT DOMINIC.

Translated from the French, with the Author's Permission, by a Tertiary of the same Order.

NEW YORK:
P. O'SHEA, 27 BARCLAY STREET.

Entered according to Act of Congress, in the year 1870, by

P. O SHEA,

In the Office of the Librarian of Congress at Washington.

STEREOTYPED BY
DENNIS BRO'S & THORNE,
AUBURN, N. Y.

In Memoriam.

F.

Rome, May 27th, 1864.

H. P. L.

TRANSLATOR'S PREFACE.

The subject of the following Conferences is daily attracting increased attention in England—so justly famed for her religious feeling and strong sense, yet so distracted by divisions which contradict the authority, the object, and the work of Jesus Christ. Many minds that know not the repose of divine faith, are—timidly perhaps, but anxiously—watching this great question; requiring, not only to believe, but also and rightly, to know why they should believe.

Humbly desiring to discharge a part of the deep debt of gratitude which he owes to the author of these celebrated discourses, the translator respectfully offers them to his well-beloved country as a guide in her present religious confusion and a support in her manifest and perplexing doubts, hoping and believing that they will be to others what they have been to him, namely, heralds of that " glorious liberty " which is the ever-blessed fruit of Catholic Christianity.

Whitsuntide, 1869.

INDEX.

The Inner Life of Jesus Christ,..................... 9
The Public Power of Jesus Christ,.................. 50
The Foundation of the Reign of Jesus Christ,........ 82
The Perpetuity and Progress of the Reign of Jesus
    Christ,.. 118
The Pre-existence of Jesus Christ,.................. 153
The Efforts of Rationalism to Destroy the Life of Jesus
    Christ, ... 193
The Efforts of Rationalism to Pervert the Life of Jesus
    Christ, ... 232
The Efforts of Rationalism to Explain the Life of Jesus
    Christ,.. 269

CONFERENCES.

THE INNER LIFE OF JESUS CHRIST.

My Lord[1]—Gentlemen:

In demonstrating the divinity of Christianity we have not taken our starting-point in the profound depths of metaphysics or in the distant regions of history, but in a living, palpable phenomenon, which has been for ages before the world; we have analyzed this phenomenon, we have shown you that under the intellectual, moral and social points of view, the Catholic Church is a phenomenon unique here below, and therefore divine. For whatsoever is human is multiple, since whatsoever men have been able to accomplish in a given time and place, other men are able to accomplish in other times and places. We have then changed the ordinary tactics—instead of starting from the basis we have started

---

[1] Monseigneur Affre, Archbishop of Paris.

from the summit, instead of digging about the foundations of the pyramid, we have examined its apex and its crown, beginning by that which is most visible, to return afterwards to that which is most hidden, and which bears the whole mass. A writer of our times has said: Christianity is the greatest event which has passed in the world. We have said otherwise, and perhaps better: "Christianity is the greatest phenomenon which has been naturalized in the world, the greatest intellectual phenomenon, the greatest moral phenomenon, the greatest social phenomenon," something unique, in a word, and, yet once more, consequently divine.

But what is the primary cause of this phenomenon? Every phenomenon has a cause. After having examined its visible side, we should evidently examine that which has produced the spectacle, that which explains and supports it. Who, then, has made the Catholic Church? Who has founded that society which rules minds by certainty, regulates souls by the highest virtues, blesses the human race by the new elements it has given to civilization? Who has formed, under a hierarchy spiritual and unarmed, that body wherein conviction, holiness, unity, universality, stability, and life, form a tissue of superhuman and incontestable beauty? Who has designed and produced it? Is it time, or chance? Is it the work of many, or of one alone? It is but one, yes, one alone, a man, that is to say, nothing; the word of a man, which is but a passing breath. Behold the artist! God has so willed it, then, that the foundation of this great work should be something resembling ourselves, and that man, so weak, so vain, should, like Atlas, bear heaven and earth upon his shoulders. Who is this man? What name does he bear on the tongues and in the memorials of the human race? I have no need to tell you: his name speaks and resounds of itself. Every man knows it from love or hatred, and in naming Jesus Christ I am but the remote echo of all ages and all minds. Jesus Christ, then! Jesus Christ! He is the artist! It is he who founded that Church whose ineffable architecture we have contemplated together: I speak of the Church under her present form, for the Church has existed upon earth from the day when God first spake to man, and when man first responded from his heart to God.

The artist found, gentlemen, it is needful to

study his history, that we may be able to judge whether the workman answers to the work, and whether, after having seen that the work is divine in itself, its divinity will receive confirmation from the life of him who produced it. In order to do this we must first learn where to seek for the elements of that life. This difficulty is not great. Like every man who appears at an epoch which is historical and rendered famous by his works, Jesus Christ has a history, a history which the Church and the world possess, and which, surrounded by countless memorials, has at the least the same authenticity as any other history formed in the same countries, amidst the same peoples and in the same times. As, then, if I would study the lives of Brutus and Cassius, I should calmly open Plutarch, I open the Gospel to study Jesus Christ, and I do so with the same composure. We will afterwards examine whether I have erred in admitting this preliminary authenticity; I assume it now, being in possession of it, subject to my returning to it by retracing our steps at a future period, in order to verify the documents and base them upon a degree of certainty worthy of the sacred object of our investigation. I take the Gospel, then, provisionally, for my historical title. You are free to make what reserve you please as to its authenticity and veracity; it is a right which I do not dispute, as I know you will also be just enough to respect in the Gospel, at least provisionally, the faith of twenty centuries, and the natural weight of that which forms so conspicuous a part of the world's history.

Lord Jesus, for ten years I have spoken of thy Church to this auditory, yet, it is indeed of thee that I have always spoken; but now, and more directly, I come to thyself—to those divine features, which are the daily object of my contemplation—to thy sacred feet, which I have so often kissed—to thy divine hands, which have so often blessed me—to thy forehead, crowned with glory and with thorns—to that life whose sweetness I have respired from my birth, which my youth disregarded, which my manhood regained, which my riper age adores and proclaims to every creature. O Father! O Master! O Friend! O Jesus! second me now more than ever, since, being closer to thee, it is meet that my hearers should perceive it, and that the words which fall from my lips should manifest the nearness of thy adorable presence!

There are two lives—the outer life and the inner life. The outer life would be nothing without the inner life. The inner life is the support of the other, and therefore, desiring to study the life of Jesus Christ, I must begin by examining his inner life. But what is this inner life? It is the converse between ourselves and ourselves. Every man converses with himself, every man speaks to himself, and that converse with himself is his inner life, as that which, from all eternity, God makes with himself in the mystery of his three divine persons is his inner life. Every man, every intelligent being, holds this inner converse with himself, which forms his real life. The rest is but a semblance, when it is not the produce of that inner life. The inner life is the whole man, and forms all the worth of man. One is clothed in purple, and yet he is worthless, because his converse with himself is that of a worthless being; and another passes along our streets barefoot and in rags, who is a great man, because his inner converse is that of a hero or a saint. On the day of judgment we shall see this changing being within and without, and the mysterious colloquy of each man being known, his history will then begin. Now, we proceed as best we can from the outer to the inner life; for, if this gift of judging the inner by the outer life had not been granted to us, if our outer life were any other thing than a permanent transpiration of our inner life, we should be but spectres to each other, we should pass by without knowing one another, as maskers who pass each other in the night. Happily, and thanks to God, there are orifices through which our inner life constantly escapes, and the soul, like the blood, hath its pores. The mouth is the chief and foremost of these channels which lead the soul out of its invisible sanctuary; it is by speech that man communicates the secret converse which is his real life. And although every man thus speaks from within to without, there are men in whom this manifestation of themselves is more especially called for, more needful, more authentic. They are those who come before the world with doctrines destined by them to become laws. For the first question put to them is: Who are you? What say you of yourselves? As the priests of Jerusalem sent men to ask John the Baptist in the desert: TU QUIS ES? QUID DICIS DE TEIPSO?[1] First of all, since you are not a man like other

---

[1] St. John i. 22.

men, tell us what you are, what you affirm of yourself: QUID DICIS DE TEIPSO?

And it is not a slight thing, gentlemen, to force a man to say what he is, or what he believes himself to be; for that supreme word of man, that single expression which he utters of and upon himself is decisive. It lays down the basis upon which all judgment of him is to be formed. From that moment all the acts of his life must correspond to the answer given by him to the question: QUID DICIS DE TEIPSO? And therefore Jesus Christ, appearing amongst men to bring them new laws, a new order of things, had to submit to that necessity of declaring what he was, and therewith to undergo the unfailing test to which it subjected him. It was to his friends and disciples that he had first to declare himself, by telling them what he thought of himself. What said he to them?

One day, at Cesarœa Philippi, he asked his disciples: "Whom do men say that I, the Son of man, am? And they said, some say, John the Baptist, others Elias, others Jeremias, or one of the prophets. Jesus saith to them: But whom say ye that I am? Simon Peter answered, and said: Thou art the Christ, the Son of the living

God." Jesus Christ, so far from rejecting these words as blasphemous, accepted them as expressing a truth which filled him with delight, and he said to Peter: "Blessed art thou, Simon Barjona, for flesh and blood hath not revealed it to thee, but my Father who is in heaven." And he then added, as a reward for the faith of his disciple: "And I say unto thee, that thou art Peter, and upon this rock I will build my Church; and the gates of hell shall not prevail against it."[1]

Jesus Christ then presented himself to his disciples as the Son of God—not as the Son of God in the sense in which we are all sons of God, but as the Son of God in its true and proper sense: had it been otherwise, he would not in so marked a manner have manifested to his apostle the joy he felt at his confession. Moreover, on other occasions he spake, if possible, more clearly to them. Philip said to him: "Lord, show us the Father, and it is enough for us." Jesus Christ grew indignant at his demand, and said to him: "So long a time have I been with you, and you have not known me? Philip, he that seeth me, seeth the Father also. How sayest thou, show us the Father? Believe you not that I am in

---

[1] St. Matt. xvi. 13–18.

the Father, and the Father in me?"[1] And, at another time, manifesting his divine filiation yet more clearly, he said to one of his disciples who still wavered: "God so loved the world as to give his only-begotten Son..... He that believeth in him is not judged; but he that doth not believe is already judged, because he believeth not in the name of the only-begotten Son of God."[2] Jesus Christ stood forth then as the Son of God without equal or rival, and in so strict a sense, that he was in his Father and his Father in him, and that to see him was to see his Father.

So much for friends and disciples. But, besides friends and disciples, there is another tribunal before which every new doctrine must appear, namely, the tribunal of the people. After having spoken in secret to the chosen ones, it becomes needful to quit the chamber, to appear in public, to speak to mankind of all ages and conditions, to those who have not leaned upon the bosom of the Master, who have not received the education of friendship, who know not what is required of them, who oppose to the word of doctrine a host of passions blended with as many

---

[1] St. John xiv. 8-10.   [2] Ibid iii. 16, 18.

prejudices. Jesus Christ did this; he heard the murmurs of the crowd around him, and was undaunted before the account which he had to give them of himself. "How long," cried they to him, "dost thou hold us in suspense? If thou be the Christ, tell us plainly. Jesus Christ answered them: I speak to you, and you believe not; the works that I do in the name of my Father, they give testimony of me."[1] "I and the Father are one."[2] At that saying, which expressed all, the Jews took up stones to stone him, and Jesus said to them: "Many good works I have showed you from my Father; for which of these works do you stone me? The Jews answered him: For a good work we stone thee not, but for blasphemy; and because that thou, being a man, makest thyself God."[3] The language which Jesus Christ held towards the people in order to make known to them the origin and mission of their new spiritual master, was, then, language free from all constraint and obscurity. He fearlessly uttered to them that terrible phrase: "I and my Father are one"—EGO ET PATER UNUM SUMUS.

But above the people—that confused mass

---
[1] St. John x. 24, 25.   [2] Ibid. 30.   [3] Ibid. 32, 33.

whose voice is at the same time the voice of God and the voice of nothingness; above the people —who form at the same time the highest and the lowest authority—rises, with calm vigilance and self-respect, the highest representation of right and truth. Every nation possesses a supreme magistracy which concentrates in itself the glory and enlightenment of the country, and before it every doctrine claiming to rule, either by doing apparent or real violence to received traditions, must at last appear. Jesus Christ could not escape from this general law of the human order. He is called before the council of the elders, the priests, and the princes of Judea. After hearing evidence more or less inconsistent, the high priest at length resolves to place the question in its true light: he stands up and addresses this solemn charge to the accused: "I adjure thee by the living God, that thou tell us if thou be the Christ, the Son of God."[1] Jesus Christ calmly replies in two words: EGO SUM—"I am!" And he immediately adds, in order to confirm his avowal by the majesty of his language: "I am; and you shall see the Son of man sitting on the right hand of the power of God, and coming

---
[1] St. Matt. xxvi. 63.

with the clouds of heaven."[1] Then the high priest rends his garments. "What need we any further witnesses?"—he exclaims—"You have heard the blasphemy. What think you?"[2] And they all condemn him, as guilty, to death. He is then brought before the Roman governor, who, not finding good reasons for his condemnation, wishes to release him; but the princes of the people persist: "We have a law," say they, "and by that law he ought to die, because he made himself the Son of God."[3] Pilate so fully comprehends this, that his Roman, and therefore religious, ear is all attention; he draws Jesus Christ aside, and timorously asks him whence he is: UNDE ES TU?[4] Jesus Christ is silent; he confirms by his silence all that he is accused of having said of himself, and what, in fact, he has said. The people who witness his crucifixion understand his condemnation in the sense in which it was pronounced; they insult him even in death by these expressive derisions: "Vah, thou that destroyest the temple, and in three days dost rebuild it, save thy own self; if thou be the Son of God, come down from the cross."[5] And,

---

[1] St. Mark xiv. 62.   [2] Ibid. 63, 64.
[3] St. John xix. 7.   [4] Ibid. 9.   [5] St. Matt. xxvii. 40.

when darkness covers the earth, when the rocks are broken in pieces, when the veil of the temple is rent in twain, and all Nature proclaims to mankind that a great event is in action, the lookers on and the Roman centurion strike their breasts, saying: "Indeed, this was the Son of God!"[1] And the apostle St. John concludes his gospel in these words: "These things are written that you may believe that Jesus Christ was the Son of God."[2]

Thus, before his friends, before the people, before the magistracy, in his life, in his death, Jesus Christ everywhere declares that he is the Son of God, the only Son, a Son equal with his Father, one with his Father, being in his Father, and his Father in him. This is the testimony which he renders of himself, his answer to that imperious question: QUID DICIS DE TEIPSO? And what an answer, gentlemen! What! a man, a creature of flesh and blood, who has before him not only the weaknesses of life, but those also of death; a man! and he dares to call himself God! It is the first time in all history. No historical personage, before or since, has set himself up as God. Idolatry had numberless gods; but it had a

---

[1] St. Matt. xxvii. 54. [2] St. John xx. 31.

supreme God, to whom none other was equal; and when the most shameful flattery decreed apotheosis to emperors convicted of every crime by their lives and of complete nothingness by their death, none saw in the incense offered to their ashes anything but a poetical figure, a last act of adulation rendered by bondage to tyranny. Mahomet, come to replace the reign of idols, did not call himself God, but a simple envoy of God. And if we would go back beyond idolatry in search of the most arrogant impostures, we shall find even in the heart of India nothing but narrations without consistency, ages without date, a shapeless abyss, in which our vision will be totally unable to discover any authentic mortal bold enough to declare that he was God, formally and distinctly, by these two ineffable words: Ego sum. Man is not capable of uttering so bold a falsehood, the improbability is too striking.

It is also and too manifestly useless, for what would it profit? What end could it serve a man to call himself God? Would he establish laws, found an empire? It is a human ambition, and I can well understand why he would not call himself a philosopher, since any one versed in history knows that whoever sets himself up as a philosopher is sure to remain alone upon his pedestal. A man, then, having great ambition would never advance such pretensions. God is the corner-stone of every lasting edifice. His name, even when invoked by imposture, serves as a solid cement; and it was natural that before and after others Jesus Christ should call himself the envoy of God. Men have often accepted that idea; they readily believe in the intervention of the Divinity in human affairs, and their faith, thus deceived in its application, is never deceived as to the reality of a Providence eternally watchful over their condition. Jesus Christ in calling himself the man of God would have proclaimed something probable and serviceable; but the very title of God, the apotheosis of himself by himself, added nothing but difficulties to his enterprise. Thenceforth it became necessary that in all his actions he should sustain the part of the infinite, that even in his death he should maintain proofs of his divine nature, and that his tomb as well as eternity should bear witness for him. Was this humanly possible?

Add thereto a third consideration relative to the state of religious belief among the Jews. That people had in their law only one explicit dogma—all the others, although they possessed them in their traditions, were, so to say, veiled and obscure. The unity of God, graven at the head of the tables of Sinai, was their chief dogma; the one that recalled and included all the others, such as the creation, the fall of man, the immortality of the soul. To attack this, even remotely, was to attack Moses, Sinai, all the treasured memorials of the children of Israel, all their customs, every object of their veneration. Now the name of Jesus Christ as the Son of God, even without destroying the divine unity, did not enter naturally into the ears of this people, accustomed by their lawgiver and their prophets to know only the God who had brought them out of the land of Egyyt, and who had so often said to them: "I am the Lord thy God, thou shalt have no other gods before me."[1]

If, then, Jesus Christ falsely called himself God, he needlessly created for himself unaccountable difficulties.

But let us pass on from these preliminary reflections, and see what account we have to render of the life we are contemplating. Whatever motives Jesus Christ might have had against

---

[1] Exodus xx. 2, 3.

calling himself God, he did call himself God; such is the fact. Before we examine whether what he said was true, an intervening question arises; we have to learn whether in calling himself God he believed what he said. Between the affirmation and the reality, between saying I am God, and being God, stands the question of good faith and sincerity. Did Jesus Christ believe in his divinity? Was he convinced of the truth of that vital dogma which he laid down as the basis of his teaching and for which he died? Was he sincere, or—pardon the expression—was he an impostor? We cannot advance a step further in his life before we solve this doubt. All mankind, without distinction of time, place, nations, laws, or religions, is divided into two ranks, the rank of impostors and that of sincere men, in these each individual marks his own place. The impostors have too often led the sincere, but their reign sooner or later betrays itself; and sincerity in regard to man is a requirement which honors him; to error, an aroma which renders it less bitter; to truth, a crown which is the first object of our search. Let us then first of all learn whether Jesus Christ wears this crown, whether he is anointed with this aroma, whether he possesses this honor, without which there is no honor. What think you? Must we place him with the impostors or with the sincere? Was he of those who have covered their ambition with the veil of hypocritical sanctity, or of those who have preferred the honor of irreproachable language even to success, and who have chosen for their device the motto of the Maccabees: MORIAMUR IN SIMPLICITATE NOSTRA?—Let us die in our simplicity.

This is the great question.

It is answered by the character of the man, and hence I may conclude that the cause is judged in favor of Jesus Christ; for no more venerable form has dawned upon the horizon of history. The simple course of time has placed him above all, leaving nothing visible that can approach it. By the consent of all—even of those who do not believe in him—Jesus Christ is a good man, a sage, an elect, an incomparable personage. He has done such great, such holy things, that even his enemies pay constant homage to his work and to his person.

It is true that in the last century there was a man who chose for his motto—designating Jesus Christ—the words: *Ecrasez l'infame!*—Crush the wretch! But this phrase, gentlemen, had not strength enough to pass the bounds of the century in which it was uttered, it halted trembling on the frontiers of our own; and since then no human voice, even among those which are not respected, has dared to repeat that signal of impious revolt. It has fallen back upon the tomb of him who first uttered it, and there, after having been judged by the posterity which has already followed, it awaits the still more stern judgment of posterity yet to come.

I may, then, stop here, since nothing is higher than a universal judgment, and since all demonstration appears weak before a conclusion which forms part of the common sense of mankind. But I wish to afford you the gratification of analyzing the character of Christ, and of examining by what harmony of moral beauties that physiognomy infinitely surpasses the most illustrious forms which time has produced.

The human character is composed of three elements, namely, the intelligence—the seat of its thoughts; the heart—the seat of its feelings; the will—the seat of its resolutions. It is the fusion of these three elements which, by its measure, determines every moral type and fixes its value.

We have no need to seek elsewhere the secret of that perfection which we find in the hero of the Gospel. Doubtless, for those who believe him to be God, his divinity supports and shines through the whole visible tissue; but without changing anything of the nature of the soul any more than of the body. Jesus Christ has nothing in himself to constitute his physiognomy but thoughts, feelings and resolutions; but the harmony and blending of these form that peculiar charm which it is now our purpose to examine.

I shall not mislead you, gentlemen, in saying of his intelligence that in character and sign it possesses that which we call the sublime. The sublime is elevation, profundity and simplicity blended together in a single trait. When the aged Horace was told that his son had fled from the combat which decided the supremacy between Alba and Rome, and, seeing his indignation, they asked him what his son should have done against three, the old man replied: "He should have died!" This is a sublime exclamation; it is the cry of duty springing at once from a great soul, and bearing us in a moment above all the weaknesses which plead within us against self-sacrifice. Nothing is more simple, but nothing is higher or more profound. God has given to man the faculty of reaching the sublime in his actions and in his writings; but these occasions are rare and fugitive. The greatest men have been sublime four or five times in their lives; such was Cæsar saying to a boatman who brought him through a tempest: "What fearest thou? Thou carriest Cæsar!" Simplicity is too often wanting to the greatest actions, or, when they are simple, they do not raise us sufficiently out of ourselves, or they are not profound enough to give us sufficient food for thought. It is the same with our writings. It is not rare to find in them harmony, grace, beauty, and, as it were, a flowing stream which bears us along between sweet and flowery banks. We are thus carried on through whole pages. Suddenly, and as by chance, a powerful emotion seizes upon us, and seems to pierce even to our soul. The sublime has appeared. But it is only an apparition; and this is why it draws us out of our natural state, by producing within us a sudden and passing shock.

It is not so in regard to Jesus Christ. His actions and his language are stamped with a continuous elevation, profundity and simplicity, so that the sublime is, as it were, naturalized in them, and no longer excites our wonder; nevertheless, its empire over the soul is undiminished. For this reason, after so many famous masterpieces of literature, the Gospel has remained a unique book in the world—a book acknowledged to be above all imitation. "Blessed are the poor in spirit,"[1] said Jesus Christ. What can be more simple? And yet how sudden it bears us away from earth! The angel who seized Habakkuk and carried him from his fields to Babylon was not more rapid. Three simple words suffice to change all our notions of beatitude, of the value of earthly things, of the object and end of life—to bear us above worldly cupidity, and cause us to hover joyfully, like the eagle, above the kingdoms of the world. "Blessed are the poor in spirit!" These words will resound throughout the world; the soul, having once heard them, will constantly recall them, and never fail to find hidden in them a powerful hand, ready to its rescue. Meditation, in sounding their depths, will open treasures of profundity, a new social economy destined to change the relations of men with each other,

---

[1] St. Matt. v. 3.

ennoble labor and suffering, abolish slavery, and make a beneficial and holy profession even of poverty. Such is the Gospel—that is to say, Jesus Christ, from beginning to end; and that sovereign intelligence cannot be better defined than by saying that it had received from God the gift of continuous sublimity.

Great minds generally exhaust their whole power in their thoughts, and are unable to impart more than a feeble and secondary action to their hearts. This is especially remarkable in founders of empires and doctrines—cold, haughty men, masters of themselves, looking down upon mankind and urging them to and fro in their hidden designs, as the wind waves a field of corn, ripe and ready for the sickle. The conception of their plans absorbs them; success corrupts them by flattering their pride; reverse sours them, and all things combine to make them scornful of mankind, which is for them only as a pedestal, erect or overthrown. Even if they do not fall so ow in the degradation of the heart, they are not permitted to raise their faculty of loving as high as their faculty of thought. The piercing glance of the eagle is not naturally given to the eye of the dove. These distinctions are perceptible even in authors. Racine—pardon these comparisons—is tender; Corneille is much less so, because his genius draws nearer to the sublime. We feel in him something heroic and austere, like those Romans of whom he said—

> "Et je rends grace au ciel de n'etre pas Romain
> Pour conserver encor quelque chose d'humain."

Now, Jesus Christ, under this head, is an ever-memorable exception, and far above successful imitation, even by those who adopt him as the master of their souls. He carried the power of loving even to tenderness, and to a kind of tenderness so new that it was needful to create a name for it, and that it should form a distinct species in the analysis of human feelings—I mean the evangelic unction. Jesus Christ was tender towards all men; it was he who said of them: "Whatsoever you shall do to the least of these my brethren, you will have done it unto me;"[1] an expression which introduced Christian fraternity into the world, and which still daily engenders love. He was tender towards sinners; he sat at meat with them, and, when doctrinal pride reproached him for it, he replied: "I am not come for those that are in health, but for

---

[1] St. Matt. xxv. 40.

those that are sick."[1] Perceiving a publican who has climbed up into a tree to see him pass by, he says to him, "Zaccheus, make haste and come down, for this day I must abide in thy house."[2] A sinful woman approaches him, and ventures even to anoint his feet with ointment, to the great scandal of a large assembly; he reassures her by that immortal allocution: "Her sins, which are many, are forgiven, because she has loved much."[3] They bring before him a woman taken in adultery, in order to force a judgment from him, which by its very leniency may compromise him; he answers: "He that is without sin among you, let him cast the first stone at her."[4] He was tender towards his ungrateful and parricidal country; and, beholding its walls from afar, he wept, saying: "Jerusalem! Jerusalem! thou that killest the prophets, and stonest them that are sent unto thee, how often would I have gathered together thy children, as the hen doth gather her chickens under her wings, and thou wouldest not!"[5] He was so tender towards his friends as to wash their feet, and to permit a very young man to lean upon his breast on one of the most

---

[1] St. Matt. ix. 12. [2] St. Luke xix. 5. [3] Ibid. vii. 47. [4] St. John viii. 7. [5] St. Matt. xxiii. 37.

solemn occasions of his life. Even at his crucifixion he was tender towards his executioners, and, lifting up his soul to his Father for them, he said: "Father, forgive them, for they know not what they they do."[1] No earthly life shows such a blending of light and love. Every word of Jesus Christ is an expression of tenderness and a sublime revelation; at the same moment when he opens the infinite to us by his look, he folds us in his arms and presses us upon his bosom. We soar away in thought, and are retained by love.

And it must not be forgotten that the tenderness of Jesus Christ, although boundless, is of spotless virginity. It is difficult for those who have received a soul apt for love to hold that precious gift within chaste limits; it is the object of a supreme struggle, in which one may be sometimes tempted to regret the gift, or to desire more liberty in its use. Jesus Christ seems to know nothing of this, he bears his love in a vase so pure, that the shadow even of doubt does not approach his heart, and posterity, which for eighteen centuries, has sought for faults in him, has never dared to utter a word of suspicion

---

[1] St. Luke xxiii. 34.

against his virtue. The character of his tenderness is that of ineffable chastity.

There remains yet one thing, gentlemen, to complete our estimation of the character of Jesus Christ, and to enable us to judge, by his character, of his sincerity. A sublime intelligence, a tender heart, do not suffice to form a will capable of great resolutions. The will is a distinct world, where, notwithstanding our views and our feelings, the helm is too often guided by a feeble hand. The character of Jesus Christ on this head is that of absolute certainty of himself. None ever ventured upon a more difficult design; he claimed to be acknowledged as God, loved as God, served as God, adored as God; it would seem that the will should sometimes have yielded under so heavy a load, and that at least Jesus Christ should have employed all the human means capable of insuring the success of such gigantic ambition. It is not so, gentlemen; Jesus Christ despised all human means, or rather he abstained from employing any.

Politics rank among the highest of these. It is the art of seizing the tendency of minds at a given moment, of bringing together opinions and interests which seek to be satisfied, of anticipating the will of a people before they have a clear consciousness of it themselves; of assuming, by the help of circumstances, the post of their natural representative, and of placing them upon a course in which we shall be borne along with them for half a century. Such is the art of politics—an illustrious art, which may be used for good or evil, and which is the source of prosperous and lamentable vicissitudes among nations. Jesus Christ was admirably placed for becoming the instrument of a revolution favorable to his religious designs. The people from whom he had sprung had lost, under the Roman yoke, the remains of their ancient nationality; hatred of Rome was then at its height among them, and, in the deserts and mountains of Judea, bands of liberators were daily formed under the command of some patriot, distinguished for his boldness or some other characteristic. These movements were seconded by celebrated prophecies, which had long announced a chief and a saviour to the Jewish people. The relation of these ideas and interests to the new kingdom, the coming of which Jesus Christ proclaimed, was evident. Nevertheless, so far from conniving at and employing them, he trampled them under foot. In order to prove him, he is asked whether it is needful to pay tribute to Cæsar; he calls for a piece of money, and, on being told whose image and superscription it bears, he calmly replies: "Render then to Cæsar that which is Cæsar's, and to God that which is God's."[1] He goes still further. He announces the temporal ruin of his nation, he speaks against the temple—the object of religious and patriotic veneration among the Jews—and he openly predicts that there shall not remain of it one stone upon another; therefore this charge was numbered amongst the accusations brought against him before the supreme magistracy.

His doctrine, so favorable to the people and to the poor, was of a nature to obtain great popularity for him: this is a powerful mainspring for revolutions. In fact, he gained such an ascendency over the people that they wished to elect him King of Israel; but he fled in order to avoid that honor, and broke with his own hands an instrument which great men would commonly have valued as a gift and a sign from heaven.

Next to the art of politics comes power, one of its adjuncts, but which may be considered with

---
[1] St. Matt. xxii. 21.

out reference to the causes that generally communicate it. Jesus Christ had nothing so much at heart as to prevent his disciples from trusting to power and from exercising it. He sends them forth, he says, like lambs; he announces to them all kinds of troubles, without giving them any other help than patience, meekness and humility. If, unmindful of his lessons, they would call down fire from heaven, he reproaches them with not yet knowing "of what spirit they are."[1] At the moment of his arrest, when he might have defended himself, and an apostle drew the sword, Jesus Christ says to him: "Put up thy sword again into its sheath, for they who draw the sword shall perish by the sword."[2] Whilst the authors of other doctrines seek a sanction from victory—rashly forgetting that victory is variable and conscience immutable—Jesus Christ chooses the cross for his standard, and protests against all triumph of power by the triumph of his crucifixion.

He also despises science and philosophy—those nobler and truer means of imparting conviction. He surrounds himself with fishermen instead of savants, and, avoiding even the appear-

---

[1] St. Luke ix. 55.   [2] St. John xviii. 11.

ance of a scientific and philosophical organization of his doctrine, he teaches it by parables and detached sentences. He leaves to his disciples and to his church the future charge of blending reasoning with them, and of ranging the whole in order.

In fine, the most ordinary skill seems to be unknown to him; he makes of his death—of the time when he should have received therefrom so terrible a check to his divinity, and when he would no longer be present to sustain his followers—he makes, I say, of his death a snare for the faith of his disciples, in promising them to rise from the dead, and in leaving the confirmation of his whole life to that test, which, if he were not God, could result only in a base fraud, or a flagrant contradiction.

I know no other human means, gentlemen, of founding anything here below, than those I have just cited, namely, politics, power, science, philosophy, skill. Jesus Christ abstained from employing any of these, and yet, confidence in himself, absolute certainty of himself, never failed him for a single hour or a single moment. This very forbearing to employ any human means proves to the highest evidence his inflexible reso lution, and the omnipotent energy of his will. Nevertheless, nothing can be accomplished without means, without instruments. What means then—what instruments did Jesus Christ employ? Ah! gentlemen, what means? Do you not see what means? It was himself, his inner force, the converse which he held with himself, the sure possession of his essence. Men tremble because they see themselves. Jesus Christ did not tremble because he saw himself. He knew that his very word was "the way, the truth, and the life;"[1] he gave it to all who came, as the husbandman sows corn; the husbandman has no more need of politics, power, science, philosophy, or skill; he has the corn, the earth, and the heavens, he opens his hand and casts forth life. And whilst human politics pursue their course, whilst power struggles with power, whilst science exhausts science, the philosophy of to-day buries the philosophy of yesterday, and the skilful are taken in their own nets; the wheat fallen from the hand of God into the hand of man, and from the hand of man into the bosom of the earth, vegetates, grows up, and ripens; it is gathered in, eaten, and mankind lives! So did Jesus

---

[1] St. John xiv. 6.

Christ; so does every one who believes that he holds the truth from God: he first lives by it, then he sows it, and the world—" which is the field "[1]—the world lives by it in its due time.

We have then before us, gentlemen, the character of Jesus Christ, as the Gospel shows it to us. With regard to his intelligence—continuous sublimity; with regard to his heart—chaste and ineffable tenderness; with regard to his will—absolute certainty of himself. Now this character is incompatible with the ignoble vice which I no longer dare even to name, so far is it already removed from your thoughts. Jesus Christ was sincere because he was a sublime intelligence; he was sincere because his heart was open to men as a sanctuary of tenderness and chastity; he was sincere because he possessed absolute certainty of himself, because he had faith in his doctrine, because he believed in himself. Jesus Christ, like the Gospel—which is no other than himself—Jesus Christ was sincerity itself, and the invincible charm which is felt in contemplating and in listening to him comes from the inmost brightness of his physiognomy, by which he is seen from without wholly as he is.

---
[1] St. Matt. xiii. 38.

Granted, say you, Jesus Christ was sincere. What then? So many others have also been sincere! Reflect a moment, gentlemen; remember that Jesus Christ, being sincere, believed what he said. Now, he said that he was God; he declared this to his disciples, to his friends, to the people, to the supreme magistracy of his country; he was condemned, and he died for that affirmation; therefore he believed that he was God. But he could not believe this if he were not God, because it is impossible to be deceived in such a matter as that of consciousness of one's own personality, without being mad. Now, Jesus Christ was not a madman, and he was sincere: then he was God. Here, by an exception which belongs to the very nature of the subject, the question of sincerity blends with the question of reality. And this is no new discovery, no vain idea of my mind. Through ages past, gentlemen, the Gospel, in proving to the minds of its attentive readers the sincerity of its hero, convinced them of his divinity without any other argument. Whilst the Catholic Church, the daughter and spouse of Jesus Christ, demonstrates the divinity of her founder by the divinity of her own characteristics, the Gospel, in another manner, proves to the children of the Church the divinity of him who founded it. And this impression is common to different ages—to the three ages of man—so natural is it and so based upon truth.

At the age of twelve, in the first bloom of life, we heard the Gospel read, we heard of Jesus Christ; his works appeared to us most simple, gentle and loving; we believed in them in the simplicity, the gentleness, the love of our young souls. But that first impression too often fades and vanishes; reason grows strong with its real rights; outward prejudices penetrate within us; inward passions are drawn forth by the sun of our ripening years, and Jesus Christ falls gradually from the altar whereupon our first adorations had placed him. This time has its day. Years pass over our bondage, up to the time when reason, become more personal and more powerful, makes us ashamed of our faith in lessons without authority, and when our very passions, enlightened by their domination, incite us by lassitude to instincts of governance, of duty, and of greater self-respect. This time is hallowed amongst all others; it is the time when we enter into order by liberty itself, by that divine liberty of youth which Providence has prepared for us, and which no law can snatch from us. If the Gospel then fall into our hands, and we read it a second time, Jesus Christ often touches us again, and with a mastery which we no longer contest, because we yield it to him of ourselves at an age when nothing any longer pleads against him but passions judged and ignorance overcome. It is this second reading of the Gospel, gentlemen, that we are now accomplishing together.

There is a third, less fortunate than the two former, because it is more tardy, but it brings to Jesus Christ the homage of man in his maturity, and has produced avowals worthy of eternal remembrance. Whilst the eighteenth century heaped insult upon the Son of God, in the very midst of that school which attacked him there was a man who believed no more than the rest, a man as celebrated as the rest—the most celebrated amongst them, with one exception—and who above them all was privileged with sincere impulsions. God so willed it that his name might not be left without a witness even amongst those who labored to destroy his reign. That man, then at the height of his glory, acquainted by his studies with past ages, and by his life with the age of which he was an ornament, had to speak of Jesus Christ in a profession of faith in which he desired to sum up all the doubts and convictions which his meditations on religious matters had left in his mind. After having treated of God in a worthy, although in a confused manner, he came to the Gospel and Jesus Christ. There, that soul floating between error and truth suddenly lost its hesitation, and with a hand firm as a martyr's, forgetting his age and his works, the philosopher wrote the page of a theologian—a page which was to become the counterpoise of the blasphemy: "Ecrasez l'infame!" It concluded by these words, which will resound throughout Christendom until the last coming of Christ: "If the life and death of Socrates be those of a sage, the life and death of Jesus Christ are those of a God."[1]

It might well have been thought that the force of that confession would never have been surpassed, whether in regard to the genius of the man who wrote it, the authority of his unbelief, the glory of his name, and the circumstances connected with the age which received it; but it would have been an error. Another man, another

---

[1] Rousseau, Emile.

expression, another glory, another phase of unbelief, another age, another avowal met, and were greater altogether, if not in each separate part, than those you have just heard. Our age commenced by a man who outstripped all his contemporaries, and whom we, who have followed, have not equalled. A conqueror, a soldier, a founder of empire, his name and his ideas are still everywhere present. After having unconsciously accomplished the work of God, he disappeared, that work being done, and waned like a setting sun in the deep waters of the ocean. There, upon a barren rock, he loved to recall the events of his own life; and, from himself, going back to others who had lived before him, and to whom he had a right to compare himself, he could not fail to perceive a form greater than his own upon that illustrious stage whereon he took his place. He often contemplated it; misfortune opens the soul to illuminations which in prosperity are unseen. That form constantly rose before him—he was compelled to judge it. One evening in the course of that long exile which expiated past faults and lighted up the road to the future, the fallen conqueror asked one of the few companions of his captivity if he could tell him what Jesus Christ really was. The soldier begged to be excused; he had been too busy during his sojourn in the world to think about that question. "What!" sorrowfully replied the inquirer, "you have been baptized in the Catholic Church, and you cannot tell me, even here upon this rock which consumes us, what Jesus Christ was! Well, then, I will tell you;" and, opening the Gospel, not with his hands, but from a heart filled by it, he compared Jesus Christ with himself and all the great characters of history; he developed the different characteristics which distinguished Jesus Christ from all mankind; and after uttering a torrent of eloquence which no Father of the Church would have disclaimed, he ended with these words: "In fine, I know men, and I say that Jesus Christ was not a man!"

These words, gentlemen, sum up all I would say to you on the inner life of Jesus Christ, and express the conclusion which, sooner or later, every man arrives at who reads the Gospel with just attention. You who are yet young have life before you; you will see learned men, sages, princes, and their ministers; you will witness elevations and ruins; sons of time time will initiate you into the hidden things of man; and when you have learned them, when you know the measure of what is human, some day, perhaps, returning from those heights for which you hoped, you will say also, "I know men, and I say that Jesus Christ was not a man!"

The day too will come, when upon the tomb of her great captain, France will grave these words, and they will shine there with more immortal lustre than the sun of the Pyramids and Austerlitz!

THE PUBLIC POWER OF JESUS CHRIST.

My Lord—Gentlemen,

Jesus Christ declared that he was God, and by his character he proved the sincerity of that declaration: therefore he was God. But is this all the proof of his divinity? Doubtless the first manifestation of beings endowed with intelligence is their word, the affirmation which they give of themselves; doubtless, the expression of what they are by their moral physiognomy, or character, is the second and natural manifestation of the same beings: but is this all? Is there nothing beyond this? And even should this demonstration suffice as to the ordinary relations between men, will it be sufficient when it is a question of intercourse between God and men? Evidently not. For it requires a certain amount of penetration, and time also, in order to judge a character; a moral physiognomy is not fully disclosed in a single day, and when God appears, gentlemen, when he deigns to come to us, it is manifest that, at the first glance, there should be in his appearance something exclusive of doubt, or discussion, or time, or even science, something recognizable immediately by all; something, in a word, manifesting openly the public power of God, and infallibly revealing his presence and action. Even as there is a certain expression of the majesty of temporal sovereignty, there should be for God an eminent and adequate means, by which, as soon as he appears, every intelligent being, not in mad revolt against him, should bend before him and exclaim: It is God! What is this mode of manifestation, which I have called the public power of God? In what does it consist? Did Jesus Christ possess it? What objections does it raise, and how are they answered? Such, gentlemen, is the vast field we are about to traverse to-day.

No being can manifest itself save by the elements contained within itself, and which constitute its nature. Now all beings, of what kind soever, contain but three elements, namely, substance, force, and law; substance, which is their centre of being; force, which is their action; law, which is the measure of their action. If we cast a glance upon the lowest in the scale of beings, upon that which approaches nearest to nothingness, we shall find in it these three elements. Thus the atom has a substance, something which adheres, which holds its place, something which we cannot analyze, but which we have called by a mysterious name, signifying that which is under and sustains what is above. The atom possesses a resisting force: in order to displace it, a movement, however slight it may be, is required, and without that movement it remains stationary. It possesses a cohesive force by which its parts hold together, a force of affinity by which it attracts other atoms to itself, for it is its vocation, as it is yours, to increase. It possesses a force of passibility by which it receives light, heat, and all the fluids of which its obscure yet mysterious and profound life has need. In fine, its substance and its force are regulated by a law; it is not alone in the world, it is connected with other beings, is subject to other influences, as its own influence is exercised; its action is measured, as the action of others upon itself is measured. Substance, force, law—all these are in an atom, and all these are in God, who is the father of the atom. God is the fulness of substance, the fulness of force, the fulness of law; he is infinite substance, absolute force, eternal law. He is yet more, he is the centre of all substances, their creator and preserver; the centre of all forces, their beginning and their end; the centre of all laws, their principle, their sanction, and their majesty.

As beings are thus formed, from the atom even to God, every being is able to manifest itself in a three-fold manner, namely, by its substance, by its force, or by its law. By its substance, thus bodies appear to us; by its force, thus the soul reveals itself to us; by its law, thus the heavenly bodies, even when invisible, are anticipated by the astronomer through the general movement that governs them, withholding or bearing them away from our view. And consequently God may manifest himself as substance, as force, and as law; as the centre of all substances, of all forces, and of all laws. For if an atom possesses the magnificent power of disclosing itself, if from its very dust and nothingness it imposes itself upon our vision, enters our academies, provokes discussion, exhausts our learning for ages, how much more should God possess the right and power to disclose himself! A being that does not do this, is not. For the vocation of every being, without exception, is to appear, to take a field of action and to act in it; and as there is no action without manifestation, to appear is to live. And as God is life, his sole work is evidently his appearing, radiating, conquering; in a word, being in all what he is, namely, the king of substances, the king of forces, the king of laws.

It is true, he now hides his substance from us men, and we may exclaim with the prophet: "Verily, thou art a hidden God!"[1] But if he withholds from us that direct vision of himself, it is not from weakness or from envy, it is from respect for our liberty and for the very intercourse which he would hold with us. Had we at once seen his substance, the overwhelming splendor of that manifestation would have taken from our soul all its freedom of action; we should have adored God in spite of ourselves, whilst the adoration which God claims from us, and which he has a right to claim, is an adoration of choice and love, springing from our soul and reaching to his own. It was needful then that God should manifest himself without dazzling our vision and making us the slaves of his beauty; it was needful that we should see him without seeing him, that we should be sure of his presence without being oppressed by it; and this is why he has

---

[1] Isaiah xlv. 15.

hidden his substance from us whilst he leaves to us his light, as the sun sometimes gathers clouds to lessen his splendor, remaining still visible in the midst of heaven.

If the manifestation of God by his substance would have been too powerful for our liberty, there was another reason against his manifesting himself only by his law. The law of God is truth, that is to say, the sum of all necessary and possible relations, of all uncreated and creatable relations. In revealing truth, God indeed reveals himself to us, but under a form which permits us easily to disregard him, because we detach truth from the living source which bears it, and because we make of it, so to say, a creation, an idol of our own mind; or, being unable in certain cases to hail it as the offspring of our own intelligence, we rid ourselves of it as a stranger who offends and contradicts us. Doubtless, God is able to raise truth to the state of prophecy, by announcing beforehand relations that will result in the course of ages between events and empires whose names do not yet exist; but prophecy needs time for its fulfilment and confirmation; up to the latest moment it remains suspended in history as a dream unworthy of our attention, and, were it to apply to events too near at hand, it would lose force, wanting anteriority. Therefore, even in the prophetic state, truth would be insufficient as the instantaneous sign of the divine presence. So that, whilst the manifestation of God by his substance would be too powerful, that which he gives to us by his law, or truth, is too feeble to produce immediate conviction.

Force then remains to God, as a means of revealing himself with a degree of splendor which brings neither too much nor too little light.

But God possesses force itself, and can exercise it in three different orders: in the physical order, which includes all the kingdoms of nature; in the moral order, which includes whatever relates to the soul; in the social order, which comprises the soul and the body ranged under the laws of unity. Now God, by Jesus Christ, has visibly applied his force to the two last orders, that is to say, to the soul and to society, as we have shown in our preceding conferences in treating of the virtues reserved to the action of Catholic doctrine, and of the social effects produced by that same doctrine, the offspring of Jesus Christ. This sign, however, was insufficient to form at once a halo of divinity for Jesus Christ, when on his first appearing among men, he had to present his credentials to them in the name of the Father, of whom he called himself the august and only Son. The conversion of the soul, its exaltation to the highest virtues, needs time, and the co-operation of man·himself; the foundation of a visible society, endowed with privileges of unity, universality, stability, holiness, needs yet more time, and the co-operation of an innumerable multitude of men spread over the field of ages and space. God does not create a society in a day, he does not even so convert a soul; and when perchance he works this last prodigy, he who has been its object, and who has the most steadfast consciousness thereof, does not suddenly become a burning and a shining light, enlightening the world with the splendor of his virtue. Men hide the mystery of God, and keep it long from the eyes of the world; like St. Paul, they withdraw into the desert, and that desert— were it even the busy throng—remains long in presence of a transfigured soul before recognizing in it the divine sign.

What remains then to God, gentlemen, as his eminent mode of appearing, his own and inimitable sign, the public expression of his physiognomy in space and time? There remains to him his physical force, or, in other words, his sovereignty over nature, a sovereignty which, in the matter and order forming its field of action, meets with no liberty to respect, no co-operation to solicit or wait for, but simply an immense energy, whose instantaneous submission announces the master of heaven and earth to every man who is not afraid to encounter God. The proper character of this sovereign act is that it requires from the beholder neither study nor science, nor any preparation requiring time or distinction, but sincerity only. It is so foreign to all human action that, at least, it confounds, even when it does not produce conviction, so that the rebel has no resource but silence against the upright man who exclaims: DIGITUS DEI EST HIC![1] Therefore, human tongues, the mysterious organs of truth, have given a singular name to the act by which God exercises his sovereignty over nature, and instantaneously manifests his presence to men: they have called it a "miracle," that is, the marvellous in the highest degree, the act which constitutes the public power of God.

But does Jesus Christ bear upon his brow this

---

[1] Exodus viii. 19.

sign of absolute force? Did he work miracles? Did he exercise the public power of God?

One day John the Baptist sent his disciples to ask him: "Art thou he that should come, or look we for another?" Jesus Christ answers them: "Go, and tell John what you have heard and seen; the blind see, the lame walk, the lepers are cleansed, the deaf hear, the dead rise again, to the poor the Gospel is preached."[1] That is to say, Jesus Christ, the man whom we have acknowledged as the most admirable character shown in history, was not afraid to give as proof of his mission and divinity a whole series of miraculous acts wrought by himself. And indeed, the Gospel, from beginning to end, is a series of simple sayings which pierce to the very centre of the soul, and of prodigious sayings which agitate nature even to its foundations. Vainly have men endeavored to separate these, and see two works in one single work; the Gospel resists that analysis which pretends to extract from it the moral substance and put aside the miraculous substance, to take from the worker of miracles the support of the sage, and from the sage the support of the worker of mira-

---
[1] St. Luke vii. 20-22.

cles. Both of these remain firmly united against the wily efforts of unbelief; the doctrine supports the miracle, the miracle justifies the doctrine, and the Gospel circulates in the world with an invincible character of unity, which permits and obtains for Jesus Christ only absolute hatred or complete adoration.

This unity is of itself a demonstration for all who reflect seriously. Nevertheless, unbelief, amazed at its powerlessness to divide Jesus Christ, falls back upon itself, and anxiously exclaims: Is it then really true that Jesus Christ gave sight to the blind, made the lame to walk, cleansed the lepers, gave hearing to the deaf, and life to the dead? Is it true that he acted as the master of nature, and that daily, before the eyes of the people, in the light of heaven, his creating hand proved that a divine virtue dwelt in him? Is there not a horrible falsehood engrafted upon the sincerity of that life?

Gentlemen, the Gospel is from a period in history: it is a history. The miracles of Jesus Christ were wrought in the public squares, before multitudes of all conditions, before numerous and bitter enemies. They formed the basis of a teaching which divided a whole country, and which soon divided the universe. If, notwithstanding the character of truth which distinguishes the Gospel from all other books, you suspect its testimony as the work of those who believed in Jesus Christ, you cannot, by a contrary reason, suspect the recitals and impressions of those who did not believe in the new master, and who everywhere persecuted his disciples, his doctrines, and even his name. A public discussion was raised, a man called himself God; he died for having done so; his nation, divided upon his tomb, appealed from that blood, and from his nation men appealed to that blood shed, which on all sides found adorers. Now publicity is a power which forces the enemies of a cause to pronounce openly, and in spite of themselves to concur in the authentic formation of a history which they detest and would fain utterly destroy. It is in vain; publicity forces them, they are compelled to speak, and even in calumniating they are compelled to speak enough of truth to save it for ever from perishing. This it is, gentlemen, that saves history. Nothing in the world is more hated and more feared; the oppressors of nations and the oppressors of God labor at nothing more vigorously than in endeavoring to prevent the existence of history; they silence the four winds of heaven against it, they shut up their victim within the narrow and deep walls of their dungeons; they surround it with cannon, lances, and all the instruments of menace and fear; but publicity is stronger than any empire; it bears along even those who hold it in execration; it constrains them to speak; the cannon turn, the lances fall, and history passes on!

So, gentlemen, has the history of the miracles of Jesus Christ advanced. It has advanced by his very enemies; by the Pharisees who crucified him, by the pagan rationalists who crucify his memory. The deicidal Jews, in the face of publicity filling the whole world, could not avoid expressing their sentiments and opinions upon the miraculous life of Christ; they were compelled to pronounce an affirmation or a denial, and a denial they dared not pronounce, because no one in the world can impose absolute falsehood in regard to public facts after the world has spoken. Absolute falsehood is no more possible in the order of history than is absolute error in the order of speculation. The Jews have perverted the miracles of Jesus Christ;

they have not denied them; they have written that Jesus Christ assumed in the temple the incommunicable name of God, and that by that sovereign name he commanded nature. This explanation is deposited in the most grave monuments of their tradition, and this is all they have been able to do against the accusing memory of Jesus Christ, against the blood which the whole universe reproached, and still reproaches them for shedding. But what more could they do? Publicity is master of men who have seen; it becomes changed into tradition upon their tomb, and pursues them from age to age, from justice to justice, even to their latest posterity.

The pagan rationalists came in their turn to deal with the history of Jesus Christ. Doubtless they had taken no part in his crucifixion, and it was not his blood that alarmed them; but, with his blood, Jesus Christ had shed upon the world a truth which condemned to nothingness the wisdom of the wise; could the wise of this world forgive him? They also then had to give a critical text of his life, and, in order to depreciate it, they had to employ all the resources which the traditions and discussions of their times afforded them. What have they said of the miracles of

Jesus Christ? What have Celsus, Porphyrius, Julian—names for ever illustrious, because from the earliest Christian ages they have been the heralds of the Son of God in the incomparable offices of enmity—what have they said of him? Have they denied that Jesus Christ wrought miraculous works in support of his doctrine? No more than the Jews; they have simply made a skilful magician of him. Why a magician and not a sage? What need was there of so strange an expression? It is because history was there. It was possible to pervert the miraculous works of Jesus Christ; it was not possible to be silent in regard to them.

It is then clear, gentlemen, by the very testimony of the enemies of Jesus Christ, that his preaching was accompanied by superhuman prodigies. But we must not separate these exterior incentives to faith, strong as they are, from the intimate character of the Gospel and Jesus Christ. In an edifice all is bound together from the base to the summit. If Jesus Christ was sincere, as we have shown, if his nature was stamped with the character of divine superiority, his sincerity and his superiority call for confidence in his miracles, as well as in the affirmations which he made of himself. If Jesus Christ did not speak falsely in declaring that he was God, by a stronger reason he did not lie in acting as God. For it is more shameful, more contrary to sincerity to perform impostures, that is to say—pardon the expression, but by its force, that very expression shows the scorn in which mankind holds imposture—it is more shameful to be a juggler than a knave. The knave deceives only by his speech, the juggler adds thereto miserable manipulations in order to dazzle the eyes of ignorant spectators. It is a lie heaped upon a lie, an indignity upon an indignity. And this is why human tongues—so skilful in expressing scorn—have created that odious name of juggler to mark all who dare to employ illusion in aid of imposture.

The superiority of Jesus Christ is no less favorable to the reality of his miracles than his sincerity. No grave and learned man will ever employ juggles to support a doctrinal teaching. For what is jugglery? It is the use of a power unknown to the science of the times in which it is practised. But science will not be slow to arrive at it; absent for a moment, it is inevitable in the course of mankind; a day comes when it rises radiant, and, casting back its investigating lustre upon the past, it judges, weighs, verifies all, and, whilst it brings to the true works of genius or of the Divinity their final consecration, it reduces to dust the puerile practices which had imposed upon the faith of untaught generations. Therefore nothing great in the world has ever been founded upon impostures of this kind; every work possessing any force or dignity, even if not altogether free from falsehood, has gathered its meed of stability from something ancient and true. Mahomet is a memorable example of this. Author of a religious revolution in a country unenlightened by science, he employed every human means to insure success, but he did not employ jugglery, because it is not a human means. I have recently read through the Koran. Every twenty pages Mahomet touches the question of miracles; he objects, or he is reproached with not performing them; never does he once venture to say that he had performed or ever would perform them; he constantly eludes the question. He invokes Abraham, Moses, all the patriarchs; an event in his life when God protected him; a victory which had crowned his arms and justified his doctrine; he loudly affirms that God is God, and that Mahomet is his prophet; this is all. And this scorn of miserable imposture, this respect for general ideas in regard to Providence and traditional memorials, is not an insignificant mark of his skill, and even of his genius.

And we are to believe that Jesus Christ, the author of the Gospel, stooped to the most unworthy imitations of the omnipotence of God, that he passed the time of his public mission in deceiving the eyes of his contemporaries by phantoms as despicable as they are powerless! We are to believe that such miserable trickery could have obtained the greatest success of faith which the human race has ever wrought! It is not possible. Common sense as well as history condemns such a supposition. The public life of Jesus Christ answers to his inner life, and his inner life confirms his public life. He declared himself to be God, he was believed to be God, he acted as God, and precisely because that position is one of marvellous strength men have been forced to try their greatest efforts against it; history and common sense speaking too loudly in favor of Jesus Christ, it was needful to have recourse to metaphysics and physics in order to snatch from his hands at least the sceptre of miracles. Let us see whether they have succeeded.

Two things are advanced against him. First, Jesus Christ wrought no miracles, because it is impossible. Secondly, his working miracles is of no importance, since everybody can work them, everybody has wrought them, everybody works them.

First, Jesus Christ wrought no miracles because it is impossible. And why? Because nature is subject to general laws, which make of its body a perfect and harmonious unity where each part answers to all, so that if one single point were violated the whole would at once perish. Order, even when it comes from God, is not an arbitrary thing able to destroy or change itself at will; order necessarily excludes disorder, and no greater disorder can be conceived in nature than that sovereign action which would possess the faculty of destroying its laws and its constitution. Miracles are impossible under these two heads; impossible as disorder, impossible because a partial violation of nature would be its total destruction.

That is to say, gentlemen, that it is impossible for God to manifest himself by the single act which publicly and instantaneously announces his presence, by the act of sovereignty. Whilst the lowest in the scale of being has the right to appear in the bosom of nature by the exercise of its proper force; whilst the grain of sand, called into the crucible of the chemist, answers to his interrogations by characteristic signs which range it in the registers of science, to God alone it should be denied to manifest his force in the personal measure that distinguishes him and makes him a separate being! Not only should God not have manifested himself, but it must be for ever impossible for him to manifest himself, in virtue even of the order of which he is the creator. To act, is to live; to appear, is to live; to communicate, is to live; but God can no longer act, appear, communicate himself; that is denied to him. Banished to the profound depths of his silent and obscure eternity, if we interrogate him, if we supplicate him, if we cry to him, he can only say to us—supposing, however, that he is able to answer us: "What would you have? I have made laws! Ask of the sun and the stars, ask of the sea and the sand upon its shores; as for me, my condition is fixed, I am nothing but repose, and the contemplative servant of the works of my hands!"

Ah! gentlemen, it is not thus that the whole human race has hitherto understood God. Men have understood him as a free and sovereign being; and, even if they have not always had a correct knowledge of his nature, they have at least never refused to him power and goodness. In all times and places, sure of these two attributes of their heavenly Father, they have offered up their ever fervent prayer to him; they have asked all from him, and daily, upon their bended knees, they ask him to enlighten their minds, to give them uprightness of heart, health of body, to preserve them from scourges, to give them victory in war, prosperity in peace, the satisfaction of every want in every state and condition.

There is perhaps some poor woman here who hardly understands what I say. This morning she knelt by the bedside of her sick child; and, forsaken by all, without bread for the day, she clasped her hands and called to him who ripens the corn and creates charity. "O Lord," said she, "come to my help; O Lord, make haste to help me!" And even whilst I speak, numberless voices are lifted up towards God from all parts of the earth to ask from him things in which nature alone can do nothing, and in which those souls are persuaded that God can do all. Who then is deceived here? Is it the metaphysician, or the human race? And how has nature taught us to despise nature in order to trust in God? For it is not science that teaches us to pray, we pray in spite of science; and as there is nothing here below but science, nature and God; if we pray in spite of science, it must be nature or God that teaches us to pray, and to believe with all our heart in the miracles of divine power and goodness. After this, whether nature become disorganized or not, or even if it must perish whenever the finger of God touches it, it is assuredly the very least concern to us. Nevertheless, out of respect for certain minds, I will show that miracles do no violence to the natural order.

Nature, as I have already said, possesses three elements; namely, substances, forces, and laws. Substances are essentially variable; they change their form, their weight, combining and separating at each moment. Forces bear the same character; they increase and diminish, cohere, accumulate, or separate. They have nothing immutable but the mathematical laws, which at the same time govern forces and substances, and whence the order of the universe proceeds. The mobility of forces and substances spreads movement and life in nature; the immutability of mathematical laws maintains there an order which never fails. Without the first of these all would be lifeless; without the second all would be chaos. This established, what does God do when he works a miracle? Does he touch the principle of universal order, which is the mathematical law? By no means. The mathematical law appertains to the region of ideas—that is to say, to the region of the eternal and the absolute; God can do nothing here, for it is himself. But he acts upon substances and upon forces—upon substances which are created, upon forces which have their root in his supreme will. Like ourselves, who, being subject to the general combinations of nature, nevertheless draw from our interior vitality movements which are in appearance contrary to the laws of weight, God acts upon the universe as we act upon our bodies. He applies somewhere the force needful to produce there an unusual movement: it is a miracle, because God alone, in the infinite fount of his will—which is the centre of all created and possible forces—is able to draw forth sufficient elements to act suddenly to this degree. If it please him to stop the sun—to use a common expression—he opposes to its projective force a force which counterbalances it, and which, by virtue even of the mathematical law, produces repose. It is not more difficult for him to stop the whole movement of the universe.

It is the same with all other miracles; it is a question of force, the use of which, so far from doing violence to the physical order—which indeed would be of little moment—returns to it of its own accord, and, moreover, maintains upon earth the moral and religious order, without which the physical order would not exist.

This objection answered, gentlemen, let us proceed to examine the second. We are told that miracles prove nothing, because all doctrines have miracles in their favor, and because, by the help of a certain occult science, it is easy to perform them.

I boldly deny that any historical doctrine, that is, any doctrine founded in the full light of history by men authentically known, possesses miraculous works for its basis. At the present time, we have no example of it; no one, before our eyes, among so many instructors of the human race whom we see around us, has as yet dared to promise us the exercise of a power superior to the ordinary power which we dispose of. No one of our contemporaries has appeared in public giving sight to the blind and raising the dead to life. Extravagance has reached ideas and style only, it has not gone beyond. Returning from the present age back to Jesus Christ, we find no one, amongst the innumerable multitude of celebrated heresiarchs, who has been able to boast that he could command nature and place the inspirations of his rebellious pride under the protection of miracles. Mahomet, at the same time heretic and unbeliever, did not attempt it any more than the others: this I have already said, and the Koran will more fully prove it to any one who will take the pains to read that plagiarism of the Bible made by a student of rhetoric at Mecca. Beyond Jesus Christ, in the ages claimed by history, what remains, if we put aside Moses and the prophets—that is, the very ancestors of Jesus Christ? Shall we notice certain strange facts connected with Greece and Rome? Shall we speak of that augur, who, says Livy, cut a stone with a razor; or of that Vestal who drew along a vessel by her girdle, or even of the blind man cured by Vespasian? These facts, whatever they may be, are isolated and belong to no doctrine; they have provoked no discussion in the world, and have established nothing; they are not doctrinal facts. Now we are treating of miracles which have founded religious doctrines—the only miracles worthy of consideration; for it is evident that if God manifests himself by acts of sovereignty, it must be for some great cause, worthy of himself and worthy of us, that is to say, for a cause which affects the eternal destinies of the whole human race. This places out of the question altogether all isolated facts, such as those related in the life of Apollonius of Thyana.

This personage is of the first century of the Christian era, and his life was written at a much later period by an Alexandrine philosopher called Philostratus, who designed to make of it a rival to the Gospel, and of Apollonius himself the counterpart of Jesus Christ. A most singular physiognomy is here presented to us, but that is all. What has Apollonius of Thyana accomplished in regard to doctrine? Where are his writings, his social works, the traces of his passage upon earth? He died on the morrow of his life. Instead of certain equivocal facts, had he removed mountains during his life, it would but have been a literary curiosity, an accident, a man, nothing.

Where then shall we look for doctrines founded in the light of history upon miraculous events? Where in the historical world is there another omnipotence than that of Jesus Christ? Where do we find other miracles than his and those of the saints who have chosen him for their master, and who have derived from him the power to continue what he had begun? Nothing appears upon the horizon; Jesus Christ alone remains, and his enemies, eternally attacking him, are able to bring against him nothing but doubts, and not a single fact equal or even analogous to him.

But do there not at least exist in nature certain occult forces which have since been made known to us, and which Jesus Christ might have employed! I will name, gentlemen, the occult forces alluded to, and I will do so without any hesitation; they are called magnetic forces. And I might easily disembarrass myself of them, since science does not yet recognize them, and even proscribes them. Nevertheless I choose rather to obey my conscience than science. You invoke then the magnetic forces; I believe in them sincerely, firmly; I believe that their effects have been proved, although in a manner which is as yet incomplete, and probably will ever remain so, by instructed, sincere, and even by Christian men; I believe that these effects, in the great generality of cases, are purely natural; I believe that their secret has never been lost to the world, that it has been transmitted from age to age, that it has occasioned a multitude of mysterious actions whose trace is easily distinguished, and that it has now only left the shade of hidden transmissions because this age has borne upon its brow the sign of publicity. I believe all this. Yes, gentlemen, by a divine preparation against the pride of materialism, by an insult to science, which dates from a more remote epoch than we can reach, God has willed that there should be irregular forces in nature not reducible to precise formulæ, almost beyond the reach of scientific verification. He has so willed it, in order to prove to men who slumber in the darkness of the senses, that even independently of religion, there remained within us rays of a higher order, fearful gleams cast upon the invisible world, a kind of crater by which our soul, freed for a moment from the terrible bonds of the body, flies away into spaces which it cannot fathom, from whence it brings back no remembrance, but which give it a sufficient warning that the present order hides a future order before which ours is but nothingness.

All this I believe is true; but it is also true that these obscure forces are confined within limits which show no sovereignty over the natural order. Plunged into a factitious sleep man sees through opaque bodies at certain distances; he names remedies for soothing and even for healing the diseases of the body; he seems to know things that he knew not, and that he forgets on the instant of his waking; by his will he exercises great empire over those with whom he is in magnetic communication; all this is difficult, painful, mixed up with uncertainty and prostration. It is a phenomenon of vision much more than of operation, a phenomenon which belongs to the prophetic and not to the miraculous order. A sudden cure, an evident act of sovereignty, has nowhere been witnessed. Even in the prophetic order, nothing is more pitiful.

It would seem that this extraordinary vision

should at least reveal to us something of that future which may be called the present future. It does nothing of this. What has magnetism foretold during the last fifty years? Let it tell us, not what will happen in a thousand years, not what will happen the day after to-morrow even, but what will happen to-morrow morning. All those who dispose of our destinies are living, they speak, they write, they alarm our susceptibility; but let them show us the certain result of their action in a single public matter. Alas! magnetism, which was to change the world, has not even been able to become an agent of police; it strikes the imagination as much by its sterility as by its singularity. It is not a principle, it is a ruin. Thus, on the desolate banks of the Euphrates, in the place where Babylon once stood and where that famous tower was begun which, to speak like Bossuet, was to bear even to heaven the testimony of the antique power of man, the traveller finds ruins blasted by the thunderbolt, and almost superhuman in their magnitude. He stoops, and eagerly gathers up a fragment of brick; he discovers characters upon it which belong, doubtless, to the primitive writing of the human race; but vain are his efforts to decipher them, the sacred fragment falls back again from his hands upon the colossus calcined by fire: it is nothing now but a broken tile, which even curiosity despises.

I look around, gentlemen. I see nothing more: Jesus Christ is alone.

Perhaps, however, you may yet say to me: If Jesus Christ wrought miracles during his life, and even in the early days of the Church, why does he do so no longer? Why? Alas, gentlemen, he works miracles every day, but you do not see them. He works them with less profusion, because the moral and social miracle, the miracle which needed time, is wrought, and before your eyes. When Jesus Christ laid the foundations of his Church, it was needful for him to obtain faith in a work then commencing; now it is formed, although not yet finished: you behold it, you touch it, you compare it, you measure it, you judge whether it is a human work. Why should God be prodigal of miracles to those who do not see *the* miracle? Why, for instance, should I lead you to the mountains of the Tyrol, to see prodigies which a hundred thousand of your contemporaries have witnessed there during the last fifteen years? Why should I pick up a stone in the quarry when the Church is built? The monument of God is standing, every power has touched it, every science has scrutinized it, every blasphemy has cursed it; examine it well, it is there before you. Between earth and heaven, as says the Comte de Maistre, it has been suspended these eighteen centuries; if you do not see it what would you see? In a celebrated parable Jesus Christ speaks of a certain rich man who said to Abraham: Send some one from the dead to my brethren. And Abraham answers: "If they hear not Moses and the prophets, neither will they believe, though one rose from the dead."[1] The Church is Moses, the Church is all the prophets, the Church is the living miracle: he who sees not the living, how should he see the dead?

---

[1] St. Luke xvi. 31.

THE FOUNDATION OF THE REIGN OF JESUS CHRIST.

My Lord—Gentlemen,

We have seen that in his public as well as in his inner life, Jesus Christ lived as God. But to live is only the first act of life, the second act of life is that of outliving ourselves. For all life has an object, and it is the accomplishment of that object which judges the life. Consequently, it is not enough for me to have proved to you even with the highest evidence that the inner life of Jesus Christ, and his public life, possessed a divine character; for if that life has not attained its object, if it has left no traces, whatever else we may think of it, it has been vain. It is needful then that Jesus Christ, after having lived as God, should have perpetuated himself as God; if he has not done this, all the conclusion we should be able to draw from that disproportion between his life and the effects of his life, would be that he was the most magnificent and the most inexplicable nothing that the world has ever seen. But what had Jesus Christ to do in order to pepetuate himself as God? He had to fulfil the object of his life, such as he had publicly announced and represented it, which was to found here below the kingdom of God. "After John was put in prison," says the evangelist St. Mark, "Jesus came into Galilee, preaching the gospel of the kingdom of God, and saying: The time is fulfilled, and the kingdom of God is at hand: repent ye and believe the gospel."[1] And, sending forth his disciples to take their part in the apostolate, he thus set forth their mission: "Into whatsoever city ye enter, and they receive you, eat such things as are set before you, and heal the sick that are therein, and say to them: The kingdom of God is come nigh unto you. But into whatsoever city ye shall enter, and they receive you not, go your ways into the streets of the same, and say: Even the very dust of your city which cleaveth to us do we wipe off against you; yet know this, that the kingdom of God is come nigh unto you."[2] And what was this kingdom of God preached by Jesus Christ, as being the object of his coming upon earth? It was himself, inasmuch as that he

---

[1] St. Mark i. 14, 15.   [2] St. Luke x. 8-11.

was to be recognized as God, loved as God, adored as God, the founder and chief of an universal society, of which his divinity was to be the corner-stone through faith, love and adoration. I ask you, gentlemen, is this work accomplished? Has Jesus Christ, living and dead, founded here below a kingdom of which he is the God? Has he founded the kingdom of souls? Is he amongst us the one and only king of souls? I no longer need to demonstrate this; during ten years I have shown its marvels to you; and had I not done so, this spiritual kingdom is before your eyes, many among you are its members and its subjects, it is a thing that speaks of itself and is above all demonstration. Yes, there exists in the world—in this world of mire and change—a kingdom of souls wherein God is worshipped in spirit and in truth, where men wrestle with flesh and blood and pride; where nothing resembles what is elsewhere to be found, and of which Jesus Christ is the author, the chief, the king, the God. And as the angel of the Apocalypse, on beholding the last triumph of that dominion, proclaimed its glory beforehand by that unparalleled expression uttered before astonished worlds: FACTUM EST—"It is done!"[1] so, henceforth, as a disciple of Jesus Christ, a son of this kingdom, an adorer of the king of souls, I say also to you: FACTUM EST—*It is done!*

This fact is then no longer in question between us; it is proved, it is palpable, it is here before us, and I may thus conclude: "After having lived as God, Jesus Christ has perpetuated himself as God." But it may not be unprofitable to show you how greatly this work surpasses all created power; and I will endeavor to do this by exposing to you the double difficulty which Jesus Christ had to overcome. I will call one of these the inner difficulty, and the other the public difficulty; their explanation will occupy the hour which God now permits me to devote to you.

The first condition of the kingdom of souls and of its establishment was that of obtaining faith in its founder, that is to say, that Jesus Christ should become for an innumerable multitude of men the rule of all their thoughts, and that, renouncing themselves in regard to their most necessary and most profound attribute— which is their own judgment — they should

---
[1] Apocalypse xi. 15.

accept that of Jesus Christ as their own, even to the point of being able to say with St. Paul: "I live, yet not I, but Christ liveth in me."[1] Not, gentlemen, that Jesus Christ required from us the sacrifice of our reason in order to establish his reign by faith, for he is himself reason, and it is he who gives us ours by a reflection of his own, as it is expressly written in the Gospel of St. John. But he had to require from us the sacrifice of our own judgment, which is a very different thing from the sacrifice of our reason. In fact, reason does not exist in us in its pure state; were it so, enlightened as we should be by a single and an undivided light, we should advance in the most perfect unanimity. Instead of this, although participating in reason, one and universal, without which we should not be intelligent beings, we mix up with it weaknesses, obscurities, habits, resolutions, numberless mysterious circumvallations which bar up its great outlets, lessen its light, and make of our reason that limited and personal thing which we call private judgment. It is this judgment, the result of our servitude and liberty, which divides men in the house of their common mother, and

---

[1] Gal. ii. 20

hinders them from founding here below, by themselves, the holy republic of truth. We cleave, in fact, to our own judgment in a twofold manner; because it is based upon reason, and nothing is more just than to hold to reason; and we cleave to it still more, perhaps, by that individuality which distinguishes us, and which is made up of the innumerable impressions which the ebb and flow of the intelligence have deposited in us from the day when we first exercised that admirable faculty of seeing, hearing, judging, reasoning and feeling. Now, by the faith in Jesus Christ, necessary to the constitution of the kingdom of souls, we must abdicate that personal judgment which is so natural and so dear to us; we must found our reason in the superior reason of Christ, we must break in pieces the personal mould—more or less false and narrow—which makes us what we are, and enter into the wide and deep mould whence the gospel has come, and which is the very mind of Jesus Christ.

This sacrifice, gentlemen, is infinitely painful to us, because, in order to tear us from ourselves, it touches the root of our spiritual being. It is still more painful under another head. Not only do we cleave to ourselves as nature and liberty have made us, but we strive also to impose ourselves upon others, to become their models, their masters, and to create a kingdom of minds in order to govern them. In whatever degree man may have received from heaven an elevated mind, this is his propensity; in the mental order, as in all the orders of action, the will of man is to reign. If he be favored by what is called birth, or fortune, or power, his will is to be supreme in them; in fine, if he be gifted in the intellectual order, he thirsts to govern minds. This last royalty is the most courted of all, and its most absolute sovereigns are not satisfied if they do not bring all minds into subjection to their own. When therefore Jesus Christ requires from us the sacrifice of our judgment to his supreme reason, he requires from us the abdication of the royalty which we have most at heart, he enters into a conspiracy, the object of which is to humble us before the most rightful throne to which we could aspire. For what sovereignty is more lawful than the sovereignty of the mind —that gift which does not come to us from chance, or election, or the efforts of others, but from our own selves, from what is sown in us by nature and cultivated by us? And in proportion as we possess this, whether by science or philosophy, so are we the more incensed against that usurper called Christ, who pretends to nothing less than to set up his mind in the place of our own, than to cause us to think his thoughts and speak his words. This, gentlemen, is the secret of that aversion which so many learned men and philosophers feel towards Jesus Christ; they are men who will not submit to be dethroned; and, naturally, they are in the right.

Nevertheless it has been necessary that, for eighteen centuries, all of us, whoever we may be, who are the children of Christ, should consent to be dethroned, to become little, to be taught, not only during our childhood, but throughout our lives; and, laden with years and honors, having governed men otherwise than by the mind, in our last moments, when about to appear before God, we have again been required to abdicate that reign of the judgment, so dear to pride, in order to repose in Jesus Christ as little children, and charge him to bear us in his blessed hands to the throne of that pure and eternal reason, who is God his Father.

None other upon earth, gentlemen, none other,

has obtained that supreme dictatorship of the understanding. Tyrants have oppressed human thought by hindering its manifestation, they have never governed it; it eludes all the devices of the most subtle rule. Sages have formed schools, but ephemeral schools, whose laws have been disowned even by their disciples. Should we wonder thereat? The disciple of the sage is a man like himself; he idolizes the idea of the master until the day comes when his own idea, ripe for an act of legitimate ingratitude, enables him to attain to the honors of teaching, and mark his place in the history of the unstable dynasties of human knowledge. The religious sects, although standing upon more solid ground, have, however, met with no better success. Heresy leaves us our own judgment, Protestantism leaves us our own judgment; all these doctrines, so far from enchaining faith, have had for object its emancipation. Even Mahometanism, like idolatry beforehand, was unable to constitute a doctrinal authority, and consequently it leaves its followers to the chance of their personal direction. All, save Christ, either leave to us or restore to us our judgment, and here lies the eternal charm of error. What do we now hear around us? What does the present age, uncertain of its course, and almost alike incapable of boldness in evil and in good, demand of Christ with supplication? Is it not to slacken the bonds of his rule, to retrench certain articles of the ancient Christian constitution, to revise the primitive pact of the Gospel, to sign, in fine, a compromise between time and eternity? But Christ smiles at those frail desires which do not spring from entire obedience to his adorable reason; between him and ourselves, nothing can exist but himself or ourselves, the abdication of our own judgment, or the reign of our own judgment: between these we have to choose.

It is not even enough for Jesus Christ to set up his judgment in place of our own; as king of our minds, he is as yet only at the beginning of his ambition; he requires more than our minds, he requires our hearts, he requires affection. And what affection, great God? A love which is the fulness of human love, and before which all history of love is as nothing. And that you may judge of what a prodigy this is, let us examine closely the difficulty which we ourselves find in exciting love during our lives.

Hardly has the flower of sentiment germinated within us before we seek in the companions of our youth sympathies which seize upon our hearts, and draw them forth from their dear and lonely solitude. Thence, in the history of all generous lives, come those youthful times, those early remembrances which none other will ever efface, and which, even in extreme old age, leave in our souls a perfume of the past. Yet, notwithstanding the strength of these young ties, the simple course of time suspends their progress: our eyes, in growing stronger, become less sensible to the beauties of our age, something no longer of childhood delivers us from that first charm which perhaps none will ever equal, but which no longer suffices for us. Affection cools into grave and virile confidence, and our soul, having mounted a step upon the cycle of life, needs a new attraction, which, in filling it, brings it into subjection. Shall I pronounce its name? And why not? There are two things before which, by the help of God, I will never shrink, namely, duty and necessity. It is needful in my discourse that I should pronounce the name, too much profaned, of the second sentiment of man; I name it then, and I say, that man rising from youth to manhood, needs an attraction capable at the same time of satisfying his youth and his strength, his need of renovation and of future. God has prepared for him love; which, if it be true, that is to say pure, should complete the education of his life and render him worthy of having a posterity. But, O weakness of our nature! the cares of manhood soon furrow our brow, and its wrinkles stamp upon it a worthy testimony to thought; what more do we need? Henceforth, incapable of obtaining the interchange of an infatuation already appeased for us, and which no longer possesses illusions enough for its own nourishment, we rest in an attachment more calm, more serene, still possessing its charm, but which no longer merits to be compared to the ardor of that passion which I have just called by its proper name.

All the resources of the soul are not, however, yet exhausted; as the offspring of eternal love, the genius of its source inspires it even unto the end. With the first shadow of age, the sentiment of paternity descends into our heart, and takes possession of the void left there by its former affections. It is not a state of decadency —beware of thinking so; after the regard of God upon the world, nothing is more beautiful than the regard of the aged upon the young, so pure is it, so tender, so disinterested, and it marks in our life the very point of perfection and of the highest likeness to God. The body declines with age, the mind perhaps also, but not the soul whereby we love. Paternity is as superior to love as love itself is superior to affection. Paternity is the crown of life. It would be full and stainless love, if from the child to the father there were the same equal return as from friend to friend, from the wife to the husband. But it is not so. When we were children we were loved more than we loved, and, having grown old, we also love more than we are loved. We must not complain of it. Your children take the very road upon which you have passed before them, the road of affection, the road of love—eager courses which do not permit them to reward that gray-haired passion which we call paternity. It is the honor of man to find again in his children the ingratitude which he showed to his fathers, and thus to end, like God, by a disinterested sentiment.

But it is nevertheless true that, although pursuing love all our lives, we never obtain it save in an imperfect manner, and which wounds our hearts. And even had we obtained it during life, what would remain of it to us after death? I know that fond prayers may follow us beyond this world, that our names may still be pronounced in pious remembrance; but soon heaven and earth will have advanced another step; then comes oblivion, silence dwells upon us, the ethereal breeze of love passes over our tomb no more. It is gone, it is gone forever; and such is the history of man in regard to love.

I am wrong, gentlemen; there is a man whose tomb is guarded by love, there is a man whose sepulchre is not only glorious, as a prophet declared, but whose sepulchre is loved. There is a man whose ashes, after eighteen centuries, have not grown cold; who daily lives again in the thoughts of an innumerable multitude of men; who is visited in his cradle by shepherds and by kings, who vie with each other in bringing to him gold and frankincense and myrrh. There is a man whose steps are unweariedly retrodden by a large portion of mankind, and who, although no longer present, is followed by that throng in all the scenes of his bygone pilgrimage, upon the knees of his mother, by the borders of the lakes, to the tops of the mountains, in the byways of the valleys, under the shade of the olive-trees, in the still solitude of the deserts. There is a man, dead and buried, whose sleep and whose awaking have ever eager watchers, whose every word still vibrates and produces more than love, produces virtues fructifying in love. There is a man, who eighteen centuries ago was nailed to the gibbet, and whom millions of adorers daily detach from this throne of his suffering, and kneeling before him, prostrating themselves as low as they can without shame, there, upon the earth, they kiss his bleeding feet with unspeakable ardor. There is a man who was scourged, killed, crucified, whom an ineffable passion raises from death and infamy, and exalts to the glory of love unfailing which finds in him peace, honor, joy, and even ecstacy. There is a man pursued in his sufferings and in his tomb by undying hatred, and who, demanding apostles and martyrs from all posterity, finds apostles and martyrs in all generations. There is a man, in fine, and one only, who has founded his love upon earth, and that man is thyself, O Jesus! who hast been pleased to baptize me, to anoint me, to consecrate me in thy love, and whose name alone now opens my very heart, and draws from it those accents which overpower me and raise me above myself.

But among great men who are loved? Among warriors? Is it Alexander? Cæsar? Charlemagne? Among sages? Aristotle? or Plato? Who is loved among great men? Who? Name me even one; name me a single man who has died and left love upon his tomb. Mahomet is venerated by Mussulmans; he is not loved. No feeling of love has ever touched the heart of a Mussulman repeating his maxim: "God is God, and Mahomet is his prophet." One man alone has gathered from all ages a love which never fails; Jesus Christ is the sovereign lord of hearts as he is of minds, and by a grace confirmatory of that which belongs only to him, he has given to his saints also the privilege of producing in men a pious and faithful remembrance.

Yet even this is not all; the kingdom of souls is not yet established. Jesus Christ, being God, should not be satisfied with steadfast faith and immortal love, he must exact adoration. Adoration is the annihilation of one's self before a superior being, and this sentiment, gentlemen, is not a stranger to us. It lies, like all the others, in the very depth of our nature, and plays a more important part there than you are perhaps aware of. Let us not disguise this truth from ourselves; all of us, more or less, desire to be adored. It is this innate thirst for adoration which has produced every tyranny. You sometimes wonder that a prince should weave together numberless intrigues in order to emancipate himself from human and divine laws; that he should add violence to cunning, shed streams of blood and march onward to the execration of mankind; you ask yourselves why he does this. Ah! gentlemen, for the very natural object of being adored, of seeing every thought subject to his own, every will in conformity to his will, every right, every duty, emanating from him, and even the bodies of men bent like slaves before his mortal body. Such is the depth of our heart, as was Satan's. But by a counterpoise due to that frightful malady of pride, we can only desire adoration for ourselves by abhorring the adoration of others. Thence springs the execration that follows despotism. Mankind, abased by a power despising all law, concentrates its secret indignation within itself, awaits the inevitable day of the despot's weakness, and, when that day comes, it turns upon and tramples under foot the vile creature who had disdained it even to demanding incense from it. A great orator once said to a celebrated tribune: "There is but one step from the Capitol to the Tarpeian rock." I shall say with as much truth, although in less grand expression: There is but one step from the altar to the common sewer. Whosoever has been adored will sooner or later be hurled by the hand of the people from the lofty summit of divine majesty usurped, to the execration of eternal opprobrium. Such do we find history—that power charged with the promulgation of the judgments of God upon the pride of man.

In spite of history, however, Jesus Christ is adored. A man, mortal and dead, he has obtained adoration which still endures, and of which the world offers no other example. What emperor has held his temples and his statues? What has become of all that population of gods created by adulation? Their dust even no longer exists, and the surviving remembrance of them serves but to excite our wonder at the extravagance of men and the justice of God. Jesus Christ alone remains standing upon his altars, not in a corner of the world, but over the whole earth, and among nations celebrated by the cultivation of the mind. The greatest monuments of art shelter his sacred images, the most magnificent ceremonies assemble the people under the influence of his name; poetry, music, painting, sculpture, exhaust their resources to proclaim his glory and to offer him incense worthy of the adoration which ages have consecrated to him. And yet, upon what throne do they adore him? Upon a cross! Upon a cross? They adore him under the mean appearances of bread and wine! Here, thought becomes altogether confounded. It would seem that this man has taken delight in abusing his strange power, and in insulting mankind by prostrating them in wonder before the most vain shadows. Having by his crucifixion descended lower than death, he made even of ignominy the throne of his divinity; and, not satisfied with this triumph, he willed that we should acknowledge his supreme essence and his eternal life by an adoration which is a startling contradiction to our senses! Can such success in such daring be in any way understood?

It is true many have endeavored to overthrow his altars; but their powerlessness has but served to confirm his glory. At each outrage he has seemed to grow greater; genius has protected him against genius, science against science, empire against empire; whatever arms have been uplifted against him he has made his own; and, when apparently vanquished, the world has still beheld him calm, serene, master, adored!

Thus has he founded the kingdom of souls by a faith which costs us the sacrifice of our own judgment, by a love which exceeds all love, by an adoration which we have given to him alone; a triple mystery of a force which reveals his divinity to us, and which will yet more clearly reveal it when we shall have taken account of the public difficulty that stood in the way of the establishment of this supernatural kingdom.

The place was filled, gentlemen, when Jesus Christ came into the world; the place was filled because it is never void. Even had he pretended to establish between himself and us secret relations only, a kind of obscure worship, this design would sooner or later have encountered fears and jealousies, manifested by public opposition. But Jesus Christ was far from desiring to hide his reign; he had said: "That which you hear in the ear, preach ye upon the housetops,"[1] and he himself, the enemy of all mysterious initiation, had constantly spoken and acted before the eyes of the multitude and the authorities. He willed a visible reign, a social constitution of his doctrine, a recognized priesthood, temples, laws, rights; and consequently it was inevitable that he should find in his way the religious and political establishment which preceded him. That establishment had two names: it was called idolatry, and the Roman empire. Idolatry was the worship that assembled the universe under one and the same religious form; the Roman empire was the power that governed all known mankind, or nearly so. The one and the other were incompatible with the establishment of the reign of Jesus Christ, and that reign could only begin by abolishing idolatry as a false religion, and by modifying the Roman empire so as to fit it for the laws promulgated by the Gospel.

You have, perhaps, hitherto considered idolatry as a religious organization easy to overthrow; you have greatly deceived yourselves. Of all the forms of worship that have taken

---

[1] St. Matt. x. 27.

possession of man, none, save Christianity, has possessed more extent and solidity than idolatry. This is because it fully satisfied the three great passions of man. What are these three passions? The first, and perhaps it will surprise you, the first is the religious passion, the want of intercourse with God. Yes, gentlemen, the religious passion precedes all others, even the passion of sensuality. For sensuality touches only the senses which are fragile, which soon become exhausted, which tire of themselves; whilst the religious want, a sort of divine hunger, has its source in the most profound depths of our being, and gathers nourishment there from all those miseries which excite in us a continuous distaste for the present life. Even pride comes but after it; however active it may be, it is subject here below to too many humiliations not to second and bear before itself in our soul a better and a gentler sentiment, that which draws us near to God, and causes us to seek our own dignity in his greatness. Religion is the first and oldest friend of man; even when he wounds it, he still respects and cultivates secret intimacies with it. Let not the state of our country, gentlemen, deceive us on this point; do not think because there are some millions of men around us who are besotted in practical atheism, that this is the natural condition of the human race. It is the result of extraordinary circumstances, and notwithstanding the irreligion of some of her children, this same France has never, for a single day, ceased to bear in her glorious womb a multitude of souls who serve God ardently, and honor their faith by works known throughout the world.

Now, idolatry, in spite of its slight doctrinal character, gave satisfaction to the religious want; it had temples, altars, a priesthood, sacrifices, prayers, public and pompous ceremonies, a very great station in the world, and the shreds of its mythology still contained sufficient remembrance of God to keep the soul from fasting and without food.

But it must not be forgotten that idolatry in giving satisfaction to the elevated inclinations of our nature did not disdain the most abject and, abundantly dispensed sacred nourishment to them. A most profound and subtle art had blended together God and matter, religion and sensuality, causing grave thoughts and shameful solicitations to descend from the same altars.

The idolator had all in his gods; whatever he willed, heaven obeyed his desires. What a masterpiece, had heaven in its turn been obeyed! In addition, the third passion of man, the pride of domination, found also in this worship, which was crudite by its very degradation, an ample satisfaction. Idolatry was not distinct from the empire; the prince, the senate, or the people, conferred the sacerdotal magistracy, named the pontiffs, regulated the ceremonies, took pleasure in covering the robe of their consuls with the mantle of their gods. Religion was country also. The fasces and the altars were seen advancing together before the republic; the fasces, the symbol of its justice and power; the altars, the symbol of that mysterious alliance which united the destinies of the state to the very destinies of the gods.

No, you will never adequately represent to yourselves the force of that institution. Ah! if a pagan ceremony were to rise up again before you; if you could see all Rome mounting to the temple of Jupiter Capitolinus, that concourse of people, those legions, that senate, all those patriotic memorials mounting with them, and all together bearing to the gods the new victory of

Rome! If you could hear the silence and the sound of unanimity, that hum of all the passions convinced of their rights and satisfied with their triumph, pride as well as sensuality, sensuality as well as religion, the elevated and the abject, heaven and earth, all at once, all in a single day and in a single action: if you had seen and heard this, you, perhaps, yielding to that total intoxication of the human faculties, would for a moment have bowed the head, and adored in the hands of Rome the antique gods of the world!

However, they were not to be adored, they were to be destroyed, such was the order of Jesus Christ. They were to be destroyed throughout the world, since the whole world was subject to idolatry. And what was to replace it? A man, humbled even to the punishment of slaves; a man, come from a country upon which the Romans showered floods of ridicule with oppression; a Jew, and a Jew crucified! This is what the fishermen of Judea brought to Rome, to the Capitol, to replace the statue of Jupiter Capitolinus! Judge, then! Here was ignominy instead of greatness, penance and mortification instead of sensuality. Penance and mortification; what words! After eighteen centuries of naturalization, I hardly dare to pronounce them before you, without disguising them to your ears, which have nevertheless been nourished by the language of the Gospel; and it was necessary to reveal these to the Romans! It was necessary to say to them: We bring you a religion all pure and holy, founded upon the immolation of the body by chastity, and not only by chastity, which is only a simple retrenchment, but by the direct hatred of the senses. We come, with the scourge in our hands, to teach you to treat your body as a slave, because it is the slave of the most vile inclinations, and because you can only deliver your souls from it by keeping it in the respect and chastisement of obedience. It was necessary to say these things to a people puffed up by seven centuries of arrogance and domination, plunged in sensuality as well as in pride, and accustomed to find in their gods, which were to be destroyed, the justification of their pompous ignominy. But Jesus Christ had so ordered it; all that was said, believed, adopted, and the reign of idols fell before the reign of the cross, in spite of the Roman empire.

The Roman empire and idolatry were as one;

but it was not less inimical to the Christian establishment on another hand. That empire had been founded slowly by the prudence and stability of its councils, the courage of its armies, the abnegation of its chiefs, until, having become master of the world, it bent under the very weight of its greatness, and lost in corruption all the public liberties which had formed its glory and its welfare. Nothing of this remained when Jesus Christ came into the world, save a few already dishonored symbols, and when he died the empire had passed from Augustus to Tiberius by a decadency which foreshadowed Nero. The orators' tribune was mute, the people consoled themselves for the loss of the Forum with a crust of bread thrown to them; the senate, mangled and decimated in its last illustrious men, opposed to despotism only the promptitude of an obedience which sometimes even wearied the insolent caprice of the master. A single man was all, and that man could hurl with impunity any defiance to servitude. One day, it pleased him to assemble the senate, that is to say, the relics of all the great Roman families, the descendants of those conscript fathers who had borne war and liberty so proudly within the folds of their togæ; it pleased him to call them together to deliberate about the composition of a fish sauce! I thank you, gentlemen, for refraining from laughter; this is the greatest insult which has ever been offered to human nature in the person of the greatest political body it has ever produced. God permitted it, gentlemen, in order to teach us how low man falls by the corruption of riches and apostacy from liberty, that guardian of all rights and of all duties. Such, then, was Rome when Jesus Christ sent his disciples to convert her to himself, and such was with Rome the whole universe. Mistress of the world, after having enchained nations to her greatness she held them enchained to her humiliations; and for the first time in the history of the human race liberty had no longer an asylum upon earth.

I say, for the first time. Until then, by a providence worthy of all our thanksgivings, God had so provided that there was always some free land where virtue and truth could defend themselves against the designs of the stronger. Whilst the east was fertile in tyrannies, Egypt possessed institutions worthy of esteem, and judged her kings after their death; Greece defended her tribune against the ambition of the kings of Persia ; Rome protected her citizens by laws which surrounded their lives with many sacred ramparts. If from ancient we pass to modern times, we shall find there the same care of Providence in not permitting despotism to reign everywhere at the same time. The present world is divided into three zones, the zone of unlimited tyranny which has nothing to envy from the most cruel histories of the past, an intermediate zone where some action is still permitted to thought and to faith; and, in fine, that generous western zone of which we form a part, those great kingdoms of France, England, the United States of America, Spain, where rights and duties have guarantees; where men speak, write, discuss; where, whilst power oppresses the majesty of God and man in distant regions, we defend it before the world, and we defend it without glory, because nothing in that office menaces either our heads or our honor!

A unique moment arrived when, with a map of the world open before you, you would have sought in vain for a mountain or a desert to shelter the heart of Cato of Utica, and when Cato of Utica thought it necessary to ask from death that liberty which no spot upon earth could any longer give to him. At that unique and terrible moment, Jesus Christ sent his apostles to announce the Gospel to every creature, and to found in their faith, love, and adoration, the kingdom of souls and of truth.

Let us see what this kingdom was to the Roman empire.

First, it was the liberty of the soul. Jesus Christ claimed the soul; he claimed that it should be free to know him, to love him, to adore him, to pray to him, to unite with him. He did not admit that any other than himself had right over the soul, and above all the right of hindering the soul from communicating with him. Yet much more; Jesus Christ claimed the public union of souls in his service; he knew nothing of secrecy; he demanded a patent and social worship. The liberty of the soul implied the right to found material and spiritual churches, to assemble, to pray together, to hear in common the Word of God, that substantial food of the soul which is its daily bread, and of which it can be deprived only by an act of sacrilegious homicide. The liberty of the soul implied the right of practising together all the ceremonies of public worship, of receiving the sacraments of eternal life, of living together by the Gospel and Jesus Christ. None upon earth possessed any longer the government of sacred things but the anointed of the Lord—the elect souls—initiated into a larger faith and love, tested by the successors of the apostles, sanctified by ordination. All the rest, princes and peoples, were excluded from the administration of the body and blood of Jesus Christ, that divine centre of the kingdom of souls, and which it was not meet to deliver to dogs, according to the forcible expression of the most gentle Gospel.

But as the soul is the basis of man, by creating the liberty of the soul, Jesus Christ, at the same time, created the liberty of man. The Gospel, as the regulator of the rights and duties of all, rose to the power of a universal charter, which became the measure of all legitimate authority, and which, in hallowing it, preserved it from the excesses into which human power had everywhere fallen. On this account, the kingdom of souls was absolutely the very opposite of the Roman empire, and it was impossible to imagine a more complete antagonism. The

Roman empire was universal servitude; the kingdom of souls, universal liberty. Between them it was a question of being or not being. The struggle was inevitable; it was to be a deadly struggle.

Now, what force did the kingdom of souls dispose of against that empire covered with legions? None. The Forum? It was no more. The senate? It was no more. The people? They were no more. Eloquence? It was no more. Thought? It was no more. Was it at least permitted to the first Christians whom the Gospel had raised up in the world to gather one against a hundred thousand for the combat? No, that was not permitted to them. What then was their strength? The same that Jesus Christ had before them. They had to confess his name and then to die, to die to-day, to-morrow, the day after, to die one after another, that is to say, to vanquish servitude by the peaceful exercise of the liberty of the soul; to vanquish force, not by force, but by virtue. It had been said to them: If for three centuries you can boldly say — "I believe in God the Father Almighty, Maker of heaven and earth, and in Jesus Christ, his only Son our Lord, who was born of the Virgin Mary, was dead, and is risen again;" if for three centuries you can say this openly, and die daily after having declared it, in three centuries you shall be masters, that is to say, free.

And this was done.

And this was done in spite of the fury of the Roman empire converting the universe into a headsman, and losing its terrified reason in the emptiness of its cruelties. I will say no more of the martyrs; they conquered, as the whole world knows. And this kingdom of souls founded by their blood, this kingdom of souls which was to destroy idolatry, and which has destroyed it, which was to overthrow the Roman empire, and which has overthrown it in all that was false and unjust in it; where did this kingdom of souls set up its capital? In Rome! The seat of virtue was placed in the seat of power; the seat of liberty in the seat of bondage; in the seat of shameful idols the seat of the cross of Jesus Christ; in the seat whence the orders of Nero issued to the world, the seat of the disarmed and aged pastor, who, in the name of Jesus Christ, whose vicar he is, spreads throughout the world purity, peace, and blessing. O triumph of faith and love! O spectacle which enraptures man above himself by showing him what he can do for good with the help of God! My own eyes have seen that land, the liberator of souls, that soil formed of the ashes and blood of martyrs; and why should I not recur to remembrances which will confirm my words in re-invigorating my life?

One day, then, my heart all trembling with emotion, I entered by the Flaminian gate that famous city which had conquered the world by her arms and governed it by her laws. I hurried to the Capitol; but the temple of Jupiter Capitolinus no longer crowned its heroic summit. I descended to the Forum; the orator's tribune was broken down, and the voices of herdsmen had succeeded to the voices of Cicero and Hortensius. I mounted the steep paths of the Palatine: the Cæsars were gone, and they had not even left a prætorian at the entry to ask the name of the inquisitive stranger. Whilst I was pondering those mighty ruins, through the azure of the Italian sky, I perceived in the distance a temple whose dome appeared to cover all the present grandeurs of that city upon whose dust I trod. I advanced towards it, and there, upon a vast and magnificent space, I found Europe assembled in the persons of her ambassadors, her poets, her artists, her pilgrims—a throng diverse in origin, but united, it seemed, in common and earnest expectation. I also waited, when in the distance before me an old man advanced, borne in a chair above the crowd, bareheaded and holding in his two hands, under the form of mysterious bread, that man of Judæa aforetime crucified. Every head bent before him, tears flowed in silent adoration, and upon no visage did I see the protestation of doubt, or the shadow of a feeling which was not, at least, respectful. Whilst I also adored my Master and my King, the immortal King of souls, sharing in the triumph, without seeking to express it even to myself, the obelisk of granite standing in our midst sang for us all, silent and enraptured, the hymn of God victorious: CHRISTUS VINCIT, CHRISTUS REGNAT, CHRISTUS IMPERAT, CHRISTUS AB OMNI MALO PLEBEM SUAM LIBERAT! And, lest an enemy should have been found in that multitude, it answered itself by another celebrated hymn, which warned us to fly from the lion of Judah if we would not adore him in his victory. After many years, which have already whitened my brow, I repeat to you those threats and those songs of joy; happy are you if you do not fly, but if, drawing nearer, you repeat with us all, children of Christ and members of his kingdom: CHRISTUS VINCIT, CHRISTUS REGNAT, CHRISTUS IMPERAT, CHRISTUS AB OMNI MALO PLEBEM SUAM LIBERAT!

THE PERPETUITY AND PROGRESS OF THE REIGN OF JESUS CHRIST.

My Lord—Gentlemen,

According to his design and according to his declaration, Jesus Christ established upon earth the kingdom of God, the kingdom of souls; he established it, notwithstanding the difficulty of reigning over men by faith, love, and adoration, and notwithstanding the public difficulty which the state of political and religious society then presented to him. But, gentlemen, to enable us to affirm that Jesus Christ has outlived himself as God, is it enough that his work is stamped with a character which can be only divine? No; for although his success was prodigious, regarding it at the point where we left it, namely, at the accession of Constantine, yet it is the lot of every power that makes its appearance here below to have its struggle and its triumph—a struggle and a triumph, I grant, not all of the same measure, but which have, at least, this in common, that they appear, contend, and reach a favorable moment, which will be called success. What is more difficult and more necessary for the confirmation of victory is to resist victory itself. A celebrated diplomatist has said: "Time is the great enemy." Has Jesus Christ then overcome the great enemy? After idolatry, after the Roman empire, has he overcome that other power, which is but eternity disguised, the power of time? At the end of a more or less prosperous career, has he not, like all the rest, felt that icy hand, which sooner or later dishonors the greatest events, and hurls the most stable dynasties from their throne? Is he not visibly struck by that slowly advancing thunderbolt which spares nothing? Such is the question which now claims our attention. In a word, I am about to lay before you the balance-sheet of Jesus Christ, and I invite you to examine it.

Why is time the great enemy? Because, gentlemen, it is endowed with a double power, the power of destroying and of building up. What was it that overthrew those primitive empires of Assyria and Chaldea? It was time. What overthrew that empire of Cyrus, vainly raised up again by Alexander? It was time. What overthrew that empire, increased by the ruins of all the others, and which we should rather call the world than an empire, the Roman world? It was time. What overthrew all those republics of the middle ages whose vestiges, surviving in marbles and paintings, we so much admire? It was time. And, on another hand, what has built up those new kingdoms whose sons we are, the kingdoms of the Franks, the Germans, the Anglo-Saxons, and the rest? It is the same hand, skilful in creating after having destroyed, and which, from the very dust where it has revelled with so much pride, draws forth substance, order, and solidity. Time destroys with one hand and rebuilds with the other, enemy alike to both, since the edifice it raises up does but sink deeper the edifice it overthrows, for, with time, to found is also to destroy.

Nevertheless, gentlemen, let us not halt at those splendid images, which only reveal to us the inimical power of time by outward appearances. Let us endeavor to unveil its secret by analysis, in order that, having learned whence time derives its double power of destruction and edification, we may consider whether Jesus Christ has not been subject to the exercise of that formidable action, and why he alone has been able to escape from it, should we at length prove that he has escaped from it.

The action of time results from five causes, the first of which is novelty. Time is always young, and yet it ages all things. Each of its steps is the advance of dawn, but it leaves darkness and night behind. Restless child of eternity, it borrows unfading youth there, but has no power to communicate it, save but for a moment, to the things measured by its course. It passes, it sheds life; but that life of to-day soon becomes that of yesterday, of the day before, of bygone times, a remembrance, a relic of the past, and yet time is not impoverished; it is ever fertile and young, causing the new to follow the old. Now, the new possesses a charm which seduces the mind as well as the senses, and which enables doctrines bearing its impress easily to prevail against doctrines become superannuated by the simple fact of their duration. Remark what happens around us. As soon as a man is able to give a new form to ideas, and appropriate them to the course of time, he inevitably has disciples. Why? Because he has said something which had not been said before, or had been forgotten. We have the passion for novelty in ideas as in all the rest, and it is not difficult to understand why it is so. Predestinated as we are to enjoy the infinite, the infinite is our want, and we pursue it everywhere. Now, novelty is the only thing here below which gives us some sensation of the infinite. As soon as we have considered an object, we say: It is enough. Who will turn the page? Novelty turns it, and in turning it, disguises its feebleness to our intelligence by a false gleam of progress, which enchants us.

Above all others, gentlemen, Jesus Christ had to fear this inclination of our souls, which arms time with a power so dangerous to doctrinal sterility. However merciful the Gospel may be, it was not to bend to the inconstancy of our mind; "Heaven and earth shall pass away," said Jesus Christ, "but my words shall not pass away."[1] It was to traverse all ages, losing daily the force of its novelty without losing any of its precept, or rather, like God, who, said Saint Augustin, is beauty ever ancient and ever new, the evangelic word was to infuse into its progressive antiquity a youthfulness which should charm the heart of all new generations.

This first advantage obtained over time, a

---

[1] St. Matt. xxiv. 35.

second remained to be gained. The second power of time is in experience, that is to say, in the revelation that results from the application of doctrines to the positive life of mankind. Every doctrine is a body of laws, which is of value only in so much as it is considered to contain true relations of beings; it is like the creation of a world. As long as that creation remains in the mind in the state of pure conception, we may be deceived as to its real merits, because it is difficult to judge a great assemblage of ideas; but it is no longer so when, entering into the domain of reality, they are required to found or to maintain a positive order; experience infallibly manifests their weakness or their falsity; for a false or powerless law is incapable of establishing durable relations, and as a house based upon false mathematical principles falls to the ground, so no order whatever could subsist based upon ideas wanting the equilibrium of truth.

Now, who had ever more reason to fear this terrible test of experience than Jesus Christ? For, with the Gospel, he had not placed in the world a society confined within the narrow limits of a race and a country, but a universal society, wherein every soul, wheresoever born, could claim the rights of citizenship; and consequently, if the Gospel were false, its ruin should have been as great as the universe, and as rapid as time, acting at once upon numberless places and minds.

The third power of time is in corruption. Everything, having reached a certain point of prosperity, decays, because as soon as man is master he wills to enjoy, and because the inevitable result of enjoyment is that decomposition of the soul and body which we call corruption. The history of all successes is the history of Hannibal at Capua. Men grow listless and forgetful, they think themselves secure, they become intoxicated with success; the slow poison of ease relaxes all the springs of their activity; and the being who is nothing save by activity, falls little by little into the shame of slumbering effeminacy. Nimrod begins, Sardanapalus ends. It is the high road of great fortunes; labor and virtue form them, enjoyments annihilate even their last traces. Religion, even more than any other empire, is subject to this great law, and above all the Church, or the religion of Jesus Christ, was firmly chained to it. For the blood of the cross had given her life; having sprung from the crucifixion of a God, she could not fail, in the days of her prosperity, to remember the cruel humiliations of her cradle. And, on another hand, the temptations which her triumph prepared for her were far to surpass any temptations until then known. She was to see the kings of the earth at her feet, to issue orders from one end of the world to the other, to behold ages bending before her teaching and her action, to cover the earth with sumptuous monuments, and see it become a tributary to all the wants of unlimited power and glory; and under the weight of such success, reaching even to heaven, to preserve upon her brow, as in her heart, the sign of penance and humility. Or, if in one of the long days of her life she was about to yield, and to feel the attack of corruption, from that very corruption she was to resuscitate her life, not another life—as we see in nature— but her own life; and, like the eagle of Scripture, recovering the charm of her youth, soar aloft with outstretched wings, invigorated and renewed by her very poverty and by the shedding of her own blood.

The fourth power of time is chance, that is to

say, certain conjunctures which do not blend with anything that genius is able to combine and foresee, and which suddenly overthrow the most ably concerted designs. History is full of these. Human prudence makes shipwreck upon shoals imperceptible to the keenest eye. It is the grain of sand of which Pascal speaks, which one morning threw Cromwell into disorder, and destroyed plans destined to change the face of Europe.

You sometimes wonder, perhaps, at a certain equilibrium visible in the world, and which keeps the strong from destroying the weak at will. Why have those great empires not yet crushed the small neighboring states? It is because those great empires have Cromwell's grain of sand against them. At the very moment when their combinations are ready to succeed and bring about the destruction of all rights upon earth, the obscure son of some peasant, in the corner of a hut, sharpens his knife on a broken millstone; at the noise of war he dons his cap, slips his knife into his girdle, and goes out to see something of what is passing between Providence and the kings of the earth. The smoke of powder opens his eyes; the sight of blood elates him; God makes him the instrument of a brilliant action; behold him a great captain; empires recede a step before him; that knife, that peasant, is chance.

Judge now how much of this Jesus Christ has had to encounter in the course of a reign of eighteen hundred years. Consult simply the history of the papacy, and see what a slender thread has held the destinies of that throne, always surrounded by enemies, yet always enduring. It has constantly had to contend against the most skilful combinations; but what is still more terrible is that conspiracy of chance, that enemy which might at any time have destroyed it, and which, strange to say, has always respected it.

The fifth power of time is war. No earthly power can avoid combat; it necessarily has enemies, not only on account of its faults and abuses, but by the simple fact of its existence. To exist is to combat, because to exist is to take from the common seat of life a part of the substance destined for all; and if this be true of the most feeble being, how much more so must it be of an assemblage of beings raised to the state of power! Therefore Jesus Christ declared "that he came not to send peace, but war,"[1] a terrible war, and upon a scale so vast as to astound our imagination. For it is the war of the spirit against the flesh and of the flesh against the spirit, that is to say, of the two elements which constitute man, neither of which can ever completely vanquish the other. When the body is victorious the soul struggles against it, and when the soul is the stronger the body watches for the moment when its yoke may be broken. But this internal struggle does not cease here, it necessarily produces a war as general as it is deeply seated. Souls unite with souls, and bodies with bodies; it is the union of bodies against the union of souls which forms the great war of mankind. Jesus Christ at the head of one army, and Satan at the head of the other; the army of the passions, pride, sensuality, hatred, on one side; the army of the spirit, humility, chastity, obedience, mortification, charity, on the other. All these are in action in the formidable regions of the finite and the infinite, in the depths of God, of the soul, and of the senses, amidst a thousand secondary causes which add to the gloom and the chances of the struggle; and if Jesus Christ

---

[1] St. Matt. x. 34.

be God, he must in the end be victorious, his form remaining unchangeable, although continually insulted, upon the venerable summit of time and things.

Has it been so, gentlemen? Can we testify of Jesus Christ that he has been more powerful than novelty, than experience, than corruption, than chance, than war, than all these causes banded together against him during a course of eighteen centuries? Can we do this?

Yes, gentlemen, I can do this; I can even show you three degrees in this triumph of Jesus Christ over time. For, in the first place, he lives, his work is before you; although it has undergone more or less of attack in that long pilgrimage under the rebel hand of time, it is nevertheless still before you. It remains surrounded by sufficient glory to attract all eyes, and to be still the object of veneration to which there is no rival, as nothing is comparable to the hatred of the enemies who have not accepted in its temporal duration the proof of its origin in the very bosom of eternity. But this is not all. Not only is Jesus Christ living in his Church and his Church in him, but, since the Christian era, no religious establishment has been founded in the world of which Jesus Christ has not been the basis and the bond of union.

The first in the order of time is Islamism. Now, the basis of Islamism, as Grotius long ago remarked, is entirely biblical. It is Abraham, Isaac, Jacob; it is Moses, Mount Sinai, the Jewish people in the most memorable events of its history; it is Jesus Christ himself, come after the prophets and greater than they. At each page of the Koran, Mahomet inscribes a recital drawn from Christian antiquities or makes some allusion to them. Why is this? Why is it that, aspiring to the honor of founding a religion, Mahomet did not base it entirely upon himself? Why, gentlemen? Because he could not. Man can no more build in the air in the order of spirits than in the order of bodies; he must however find a basis. Now, according to the expression of Fontenelle, "the Christian religion is the only religion which possesses proofs," and wherever it has appeared with the authority of its history, error must take its support and be grafted into that mighty trunk which alone throws out its roots in antiquity. Mahomet lived in an age and in a land already impregnated with the sap of Christianity; he touched Abyssinia, a great seat of Christendom, Egypt, a metropolitan church, Judæa, where all the great Christian mysteries were accomplished; the blood of his people remounted with omnipotent celebrity to the blood of Abraham; he could only, in such conditions, found a heresy, or, if you prefer it, establish himself upon Jesus Christ by an infidelity which still rendered immense homage to him. This is why Mussulmans have always permitted Christians to live in their territory, and adore Jesus Christ, not from toleration resulting from fear, but from respect for the common traditions of the two religions and the formal recommendations of the Koran. There has been a struggle for supremacy between Mussulmans and Christians; but there has been no persecution, properly so called, of Christians by Mussulmans. Ishmael reclaimed only his right of primogeniture over Isaac. And this, gentlemen, explains to you the strange spectacle which Constantinople now presents to us, where, although the penalty of death is decreed against any Christian who should convert a Mussulman, Christians of every communion have nevertheless full liberty to exercise their worship, even publicly.

After Islamism came the Greek schism. Now

the Greek schism is the whole Catholic Church save two points—the supremacy of the sovereign Pontiff and the procession of the Holy Ghost. All the rest, dogmas, morals, sacraments, hierarchy, customs, have been preserved by the descendants of Photius. They have rejected the vicar of Jesus Christ, but they have not rejected Jesus Christ. Jesus Christ is the object of their faith, their love, and their adoration, the cornerstone of their religious edifice.

It is the same, although in a minor degree, with Protestantism. Protestantism has denied the Church, but not Jesus Christ. Jesus Christ remains the doctor and king of souls, and even for a great number of Protestants he is still the only Son of God, worthy as such of supreme adoration.

No other religious establishment has been raised up in the world since the Christian era. Brahminism and Buddhism were anterior to Jesus Christ; and if some movement was visible in the last of these at a nearer epoch, it was owing to the intercourse between Christians and the distant regions of India and Tartary. Thus, in the mountains of Thibet, since our celebrated embassies of the middle ages, a puerile imitation of the papacy has been witnessed. Jesus Christ no sooner dawned upon the world than his light caused the clouds of false religions to recede; many have entirely disappeared, and none has been formed but upon his name and history. He has become the trunk of error as well as of truth, and whoever totally denies him opens an abyss for himself where nothing but death will ever fructify. His tomb is now the centre of the religious world; Mussulmans, Greeks, Protestants, Catholics, guard it. All gathered together from the four winds of heaven, agree to venerate the inanimate stone upon which the mangled body of Christ for three days and nights reposed. A hundred battles have been fought around it; the destinies of the world have a score of times changed their aspect there; but defeat or victory has ever borne to it the homage of nations, and so many struggles have but served to glorify that fragile tomb where all come to prostrate themselves. If Catholics alone had guarded it, it would have been an ordinary protection, like all the rest that is measured by the sword; it was more fitting to the designs of God that Jerusalem "should be trodden under foot of nations,"[1] as

---

[1] Isaiah v. 5.

the Gospel had foretold, and that the Holy Sepulchre, held up by a thousand hands, should appear amidst all the events as the indicative sign that no religious establishment is thenceforth possible save on condition of participating in Christ by something at least of his blood, his doctrine, and his memory.

Time, gentlemen, will bring you new proofs of this. You will see the fading away of the miserable vestiges of religions without foundation, as the civilization advances of which Jesus Christ is the creator and the head. Fable cannot keep ground against history, antiquity empty against antiquity filled, the vague against the certain, death against life. Jesus Christ pursues his course even by the very unfaithfulness which pride brings to him; he makes use of schisms and heresies as of tainted water which still contains him for a multitude of souls armed against poison by the simplicity of ignorance and good faith. But at the same time — and this is his third triumph over time — he maintains incorruptible and above all his true Church, the Catholic, Apostolic, Roman Church. He ensures to her even a numerical superiority; for Islamism counts but a hundred millions of followers, the

Greek schism sixty millions, Protestantism a like number, whilst the Catholic Church holds a hundred and sixty millions of souls subject to her government. Hierarchical superiority; for neither Islamism, nor the Greek schism, nor Protestantism has been able to create a papacy. Superiority of independence; for no spiritual community has been able to preserve inviolable the sanctuary of the soul, save the Catholic Church, which, by constantly giving her inexhaustible blood for that cause, has kept her teaching and her action free from the yoke, and has merited the honor of being here below the bulwark of right and the virgin soil of holy liberty.

I shall not enlarge further, gentlemen, upon the marks of the true Church of Jesus Christ. I have already done this, and I hastily refer to it now only to demonstrate the sovereign providence by which Jesus Christ has maintained them on the brow of his Church against all the efforts of time.

Thus then a threefold perpetuity is acquired for Jesus Christ from the scrutiny to which we have subjected him; perpetuity of life, perpetuity of exclusive irradiation of life, perpetuity of superiority in life.

But you may reply: This is not questioned. Jesus Christ has lived; he has infused his life into all religious establishments which have come after him, and he has even maintained his Church above all the rest. Yet do you not now perceive signs of decadency in his work? Have not a multitude of souls emancipated themselves from his rule? And when signs of decrepitude begin to appear, may we not foresee a near and an inevitable dissolution?

This may be your idea, gentlemen; mine is that Jesus Christ is at the apogee of his glory and power; and this, with the help of God, I shall now proceed to show you.

Three things constitute power, and the progress of these three things constitutes the progress of power, namely, the territorial state, the numerical state, and the moral state. Now, I affirm that, under this threefold relation, Jesus Christ has never attained a higher point than that at which we at present contemplate him.

In the first place, what was the territorial state of Jesus Christ under Constantine? It was nearly included even in the boundaries of the empire, between the Rhine, the Euphrates and the Atlas. If it passed beyond, that addition was compensated for by the many parts of the empire of which the Gospel held but an imperfect and uncertain possession. But what do you now see? It is true Jesus Christ has lost some of his former territories, now occupied by Mussulmans; although it must be remarked that Christians exist upon the whole surface of the Islamic soil, and that Islamism itself recognizes Jesus Christ and his ancestors. But turn your eyes to the west, to the east, to the north, to the south, and in every direction of the globe you will find the conquering steps of the Saviour. He has crossed the Rhine; he has subjected Germany, Poland, all the Russias, the three kingdoms of Great Britain, and has borne even to the pole, across the mountains and ices of Sweden, the sun of his dominion. The Atlantic Ocean opened before him; he has passed the Cape of Good Hope, has joined to the sceptre of his children that famous peninsula of India, which from antiquity was looked upon as the reservoir of all the treasures of nature. He has founded establishments along the coast of Africa, and rejoined by the Red Sea his old possessions of Abyssinia. He has made the tour of the two Americas, and from one pole to the other, ranging them under his laws, he has raised up together republics, missions, and bishoprics. He has retaken Spain from Mahomet, and everywhere shaken the territory of Islam. But yesterday, again, when the chief of the house of Bourbon was descending from the throne and about to carry his noble old age into exile, we saw Jesus Christ, by the arm of the old Frank king who thus wrote his testament among us, conquer two kingdoms from infidelity, the kingdoms of Greece and Algeria. Still more recently, China has opened to him her ports, which had so long been shut; New Holland becomes peopled under the shadow of his cross; the islands of Oceania transform their savage inhabitants into humble and meek adorers of his Gospel. There are no longer any seas, or solitudes, or mountains, or inaccessible places where Jesus Christ does not hoist the bold standards of his children blended with his own.

Return now back to Constantine; weigh the Christian world of that epoch with the Christian world of the present time, and judge of the territorial progress which Jesus Christ has made.

It is the same with the numerical state. I said just now that the Catholic Church counts a hundred and sixty millions of children, the Greek schism sixty millions, Protestantism sixty millions more. This is a total of two hundred and eighty millions of men who acknowledge Jesus Christ for their Saviour and their spiritual head. Doubtless, there are some among these who do not bear his yoke from clear and positive conviction; but the Christian's life must be judged as a whole, and especially at the hour of death. Among the many who think themselves unbelievers there are few who resist Christ to the last, and who do not ask him to forgive their errors much more than their apostacy. Their soul, moreover, was formed by the Gospel, and it is still their nourishment even when they think they despise it. The numerical state of Jesus Christ was never more flourishing, and it daily tends to increase by the development of Christian populations. Whilst the Mahometan races become impoverished and the remains of the idolatrous nations vegetate in their immobility, the Christian blood, blessed by God, prospers beyond measure, and continual emigrations carry its superabundance into distant lands, and with it the precious seeds of faith.

If you perceive a disproportion between the territory and the population of Jesus Christ, it is easy to be explained. The power of Christians grows yet faster than their blood; they conquer and govern space with a handful of men, and their genius fills it long before their posterity. I do not think this observation is prejudicial to Jesus Christ. But there is another which you certainly expect from me, and which I also expect from you. Whatever may be the state, say you, of the territorial and numerical progress of Jesus Christ—a phenomenon which may be explained by the ascendancy of the Christian races—you cannot deny the invasion and progress of unbelief in the very midst of Christianity. If Jesus Christ has overthrown the religions which were before his own, unbelief, more powerful than he, overthrows in its turn the work which he had built up, and overthrows it with still more terrible effects, since it is doubt and negation which take the place of faith. Like those lands exhausted by a substance that has devoured all their sap, and which can no longer produce anything, the land over which Christ has passed is a land cursed, it no longer produces anything but doubt and negation. Thus we advance to a state worse than any of which mankind has been the witness and the victim. Like that conqueror who caused Jerusalem to be razed and salt to be cast upon its ruins, Christ has exhausted the convictions of the human race, and cast upon its intelligence the salt of absolute unbelief. Woe to us, doubtless, woe to us who can no longer believe! But to whom do we owe that incapacity, if not to the tyranny of Christ, who has not been powerful enough to bend forever our minds to his dogmas, and who is powerful enough to keep us from ever holding any other faith than his own?

I grant, gentlemen, that after seventeen centuries during which Jesus Christ was not denied, he was at length denied in the last century; he is denied even now. But so far from that accident menacing the work of Christ, it derives a glory therefrom, which it will be easy for you to recognize and appreciate. Three countries formed the seat of the total revolt against Jesus Christ —England, France and Germany. As to England, unbelief has long ago ceased to possess any power or renown there. If your ears are attentive to the echoes of the British Parliament, that highest of all expression of national opinions, you will not have heard, since the birth of the present century, a single word of insult or menace to Christ. England has emancipated Catholics; she has recalled to the tribune of her Parliament the proscribed voices of the defenders of the papacy; she has opened her fields to the labor of monks, and her schools to the learning of the Roman clergy. The old walls of Oxford have heard the most celebrated doctors of Anglicanism speaking of Jesus Christ like the ancient Church, they have witnessed the retreat of many who have passed from the rostrum to the humble cell, there to recite the office after the manner of the religious orders, and to pray at the foot of a crucifix for the return of their soul and of their country to the old faith of the Anglo-Saxons. Catholic churches, and even cathedrals, have risen up full of splendor from the land of proscription, and Jesus Christ has marched triumphantly with his bishops and priests in the very places where stones and the sword had pursued him. In fine, England is won back from unbelief, she who was the first to shelter it under the protection of her nobles and her men of genius.

If we turn next to France, doubtless we shall not find there in the same fulness the signs of a return to faith. Yet none of you, knowing the history of the past and the present, would compare the two positions. In the last century, unbelief was absolute mistress of minds, alone it guided the pen and spoke with eloquence; its books were public events, its great men ranked with the old families of the monarchy, and held familiar intercourse with all the kings of Europe; a flagrant and an overwhelming conspiracy hurled to heaven every insult against Jesus Christ. Is it so now, gentlemen? Has not Jesus Christ his writers, his orators, his party, his youth, his glory, among us? And if unbelief still exists, do we not well know how to make it bend before us, and how to march on in the strength of our souls against its now decrepit successes and its ill-judged expectations? We do, gentlemen; the watchword of the faith in all its most militant action comes from France; our missionaries, our sisters of charity, our brothers of the Christian schools, bear it to the ends of the world, and whoever loves Jesus Christ upon earth keeps his hand upon our heart to feel there the pulsations of faith, and to thank the God who strikes and who heals.

I shall say nothing of Germany; she remains, doubtless, although with certain modifications, the seat of the war against Jesus Christ. Our unbelievers go there to seek the arms which the genius of France refuses to them yet more and more; but the fall is great, and the thunder that comes from the clouds of the Rhine is not destined to produce such effects as that double voice of England and France, whose future alliance in favor of the Church and Jesus Christ the great Comte de Maistre has long ago foretold.

However, gentlemen, let us not be content with proving by facts the progressive decrease of the forces of unbelief; let us endeavor to trace its causes in order to draw conclusions which may embrace the future as well as the past.

God, then, seeing the darkness of men's minds, has caused three suns to rise slowly upon the horizon of the Church: the sun of history, the sun of science, and the sun of liberty. History was ill-understood; great research, aided by great social revolutions, has enlightened its sombre mysteries, and Jesus Christ, calumniated in the works of his Church, has retaken in the realities of the world a place which men willed to dishonor. Whilst history returned to him by the labors of Protestants and unbelievers, as much as by those of Catholics, science did not serve him with a lesser return of justice and fidelity. Did it dig in the bowels of the earth, it found again there the first page of Moses; did it descend to the foundations of the temples and monuments of Egypt, it found there the points of junction between Egyptian history and the history of the people of God; did it succeed in deciphering the language of hieroglyphics, those signs, recalled to the vigor of their expression, bore testimony to the newness of the world, compromised by the calculations of astronomy; did it discover and bring to light ruins and inscriptions, those ruins and those inscriptions spoke for us; nature interrogated in every sense, gave back a Christian note from all its pores, as if it had been created or charmed by Jesus Christ.

Liberty also has rendered us signal services. It has loosened the bonds with which unbelief had bound the Church by the hand of kings, and permitted Jesus Christ to resume the sceptre of speech, too long enfeebled from respect which was no longer merited.

Unbelief has, however, received a heavier blow than all these. For the causes I have just enumerated act only in the higher ranks of the world; they do not strike at the heart of the human race, and that central shock is necessary to all extended action. The centre of the world, the heart of the human race, is the people. The people then should have had a sign against unbelief, and that sign was given to them in order that nothing might be wanting to the causes of salvation which God prepares for us. What sign then was given to the people? What sign, gentlemen? It is this: the soul and the body of the people have gained nothing from unbelief, and they know it. The people had a God in heaven; when the earth, so sparing towards them, overtasked their strength, they clasped their hands, and in looking upwards and in appealing to God from their very wretchedness, they felt dignity and consolation reaching to them. The people had a God, not only in heaven, but nearer to them, a God who had become man and was poor, who was born in a stable, whose body had been laid upon straw, and who had suffered in this life more than they. The people had a God, not in heaven only, not only in the flesh and in poverty, but they had a God upon the same cross which they themselves bear, and when they beheld themselves with their two arms extended in their suffering, they found on their right hand their God who was crucified for them, and who bore them company. The people had a God, not only in heaven, not only in their flesh, in their poverty, and in their own cross, but they had a God living in the Church to teach, to protect, and to console them; they had a God living in their priest to receive the oppressive secrets of their hearts; they had a God living in the sister of charity to bind up their wounded limbs when they could no longer serve them, and to honor their souls in the miseries of their bodies. The people had a God in heaven and upon earth: you have taken away from them the God of heaven, and you have not preserved for them the God of earth. What then did you give them in his stead? What other God have you made for them? Ah! I am wrong, for God you have given them doubt, and for goddess negation! You said to them: "Perhaps!" And finding that too much, you spoke again with authority, and said: No! Why should they complain? There is no longer any God, or Christ, or Gospel, or Church; but you remain to them, and with you the worms which brought them into the world, and the worms which will prey upon their dead bodies. Is not this enough to satisfy a soul?

Perhaps, unable to bear the sight of that merciless spoliation wrought by your hands, you will turn to the bodies of the people and boast of what they owe to you, for the temporal wellbeing which you have procured for them in exchange for what they have lost. Ah! I expected as much from you! The bodies of the people! But listen to the sounds which rise from Manchester, Birmingham, Flanders, the cry, not of poverty and want—they are the words and things of bygone times—but the cry of pauperism; that is to say, the cry of distress having reached the state of system and power, and rising, by an unexpected malediction, from the very development of wealth itself. The political economy of unbelief has been destroyed by facts upon every seat of human enterprise and activity; it still struggles against these results, as terrible as they were unlooked for; but it is the hydra of Lerne against the arm of Hercules; the blow which it has received is a mortal blow because it has been dealt by the hand of the people!

In a word, the bodies and the souls of the people have gained nothing from unbelief, and the people know it.

But if you have done nothing as yet for the

souls and bodies of the people, perhaps it is to come, perhaps you will some day set up a doctrine in the place of the doctrine of Christ! I must deprive you of that last hope; and without even trusting to the nothingness of your past efforts, I must show you that it is impossible for you to found a doctrine. In fact, unbelief rests upon two general principles, of which this is the first: man should not believe in man, because one man is as good as another, and his most precious treasure is the independence of his mind. Your second principle is: man should not believe in God, because God does not speak to man. But if man ought neither to believe in God nor in man, in whom then should he believe? Your answer is: in himself, and in himself alone. Now wherever men believe only in themselves, there are no disciples; where there are no disciples, there is no master; where there is no master, there is no unity; where there is no unity, there is no doctrine. You would not then found a doctrine, even had you a thousand years multiplied by another thousand before you. If you quit the principles of unbelief, at that very moment you fall back upon Jesus Christ, the only possible master for whosoever acknowledges an authority, because without him there is nothing which holds together upon any foundation.

But after all let us admit that you may found a doctrine. Even should you succeed it would not be sufficient to dethrone Jesus Christ; your doctrine must be more perfect than that of Jesus Christ. Now listen to what I have just experienced. Three months ago I read for your sake the author who in this age seems to have had the distinction of writing against Jesus Christ with the greatest boldness, if not with the greatest ability, I mean Dr. Strauss. After having, with heated forehead, waded through four large volumes of transcendental weariness, as the Germans say, I reached, at length, the last chapter, entitled *Conclusion*. There Dr. Strauss, starting from the idea that Jesus Christ is completely vanquished, asks himself whether some man, capable of equalling and even of surpassing Jesus Christ, will not appear upon the empty stage of mankind. That question asked, a kind of tardy and eloquent justice seizes upon the author, and, in a page which I read again more than once, the only one in which the soul makes itself felt, he declares that it is not probable that any man will ever be able to equal Jesus Christ, but he is absolutely certain that no man will ever surpass him.

Such is the conclusion.

To sum up, gentlemen, I find in Jesus Christ a threefold perpetuity: perpetuity in his life, perpetuity in the exclusive irradiation of his life, perpetuity in the superiority of his life. I also find in him a threefold progress: progress in the territorial state, progress in the numerical state, progress in the moral state. Jesus Christ has then overcome time; he has overcome the great enemy, and, beholding him upon the summit of ages in all the serenity of his imperturbable youth, I remember what Saint Paul said of him in another sense: "Christ risen from the dead, dieth no more."[1] Once he descended into the tomb; but the human race, for whom he died, bent towards him, and, raising him up with a love which has never grown cold, bears him in its hands, risen again to life. Behold him, gentlemen, examine him well, he lives! Look again, he dieth no more, he is young, he is King, he is God! He lived as God, he has outlived himself as God; to-morrow I will show you that he pre-existed as God. Nothing will then be wanting

---

[1] Rom. vi. 9.

to that threefold act of life—living, surviving, pre-existing; nothing will be found in him which is not stamped with the seal of divinity, and which hinders me from proclaiming with the sovereignty of certainty that other expression of Saint Paul: "Jesus Christ was yesterday, he is to-day, and the same forever!"[1]

---

[1] Heb. xiii. 8.

THE PRE-EXISTENCE OF JESUS CHRIST.

My Lord—Gentlemen,

All life is not yet comprised in living and in outliving that life; the third act of life, which is the first in the order of time, is that of preexistence. Every being, save God, pre-exists in its germ, and man in particular pre-exists in his ancestors. No one appears here below whose reign has not been prepared long beforehand; and the more important the destiny designed for him by Providence, the more important also is the preparatory action of his ancestors. Jesus Christ, as man, should therefore have pre-existed after the manner of men; and, inasmuch as he was greater than all men by his destiny, he should also have pre-existed in a manner peculiar to himself alone. I remark then, in the first place, that alone amongst all the great names, he possesses an authentic genealogy which remounts from him even to the father of the human race, and that he is thus, undoubtedly, the first gentleman in the world. It is but little, I grant, and therefore his pre-existence should not be limited to this alone.

Ancestry, we have said, is proportionate to posterity. Whosoever has no ancestry will have no posterity, and this explains to you the weakness of doctrines which unceasingly appear and disappear before you. They begin in the man who advances them, and, beginning with him, they die with him. As soon as a man without antecedents in his teaching, a man, the last who has sprung up in this world, dares to bring to mankind doctrines which he calls new, that single word is the foreboding of his powerlessness and the expression of his condemnation. For if the doctrines claimed by him as his own possessed any importance, they would inevitably have pre-existed him, he would at most be but their renovator; to say that an important thing begins in one's self, is to take nothingness for starting point, for horizon, and for end.

But if ancestry be proportionate to posterity, it follows that Jesus Christ must have pre-existed in his ancestors with incomparable greatness. And, to speak more precisely, since Jesus Christ has had for his posterity the most important social and religious work of the times which have followed him, he should also have had for his ancestry the most important social and religious work of the times which preceded him. The Catholic Church being the fruit of his coming, we must find before his coming something that worthily prepares the Catholic Church, and that comprises Jesus Christ between a past and a future—doubtless not of equal proportions, but so balanced that that which preceded him was beyond all comparison with the rest, as well as that which followed him. The Jewish people, gentlemen, fulfil these conditions. The Jewish people was the most important social and religious work of the times preceding Jesus Christ, as the Catholic Church is the most important social and religious work of later times; and, as Jesus Christ is the soul of the Catholic Church, in which his life is perpetuated, so he was the soul of the Jewish people in whom he pre-existed. I must explain this double proposition to you, and so succeed in surrounding the sacred head of Christ with all the promulgatory rays of his divinity.

That the Jewish people was the greatest social and religious work of antiquity, I shall not, I think, have much difficulty in proving. Let us begin by its superiority in the social point of view. Legislation is the highest element of the life of a people, and, in legislation, the first point to consider is the constitution of the law itself. Now the Hebrew law possesses two characters which belong to it alone, and which place it beyond all comparison, they are universality and immutability. It has for its basis something universal, namely, the general relations of man with God and with mankind. The tables of Sinai, which form its prologue and its fundamental page, exist even now as the most memorable expression of all the great duties; and the Catholic Church, even after the promulgation of the Gospel, has not been able to substitute in place of the Decalogue anything which she has judged worthy to set it aside. Those ten decrees form the basis of Christian morals, as they formed the basis of Hebrew morals. In the second place, the Jewish law, although including the whole political, civil, criminal, commercial, judicial, and even ceremonial order— things essentially variable in their nature—was endowed with an immutability of which there is no other example in any legislation whatsoever. In Moses the legislative power of the Hebrews began and ended. Whilst every human society has in its centre a permanent legislative power which retrenches, adds, corrects, according to times and necessities, and an exceptional legislative power, which goes so far as to reform even the constitution itself, affected by the change of habits and customs, the Jewish people, from Moses, remained contented in regard to law, with a simple regulating faculty. The hand that had graven the tables of Sinai and penned that vast legislation comprised in the Pentateuch was strong enough permanently to consolidate a whole nation, how long soever it might endure; and three thousand years passed over his work have never once borne to it the slightest contradiction. Above all others, gentlemen, after the last fifty years of our history, we can appreciate the superhuman genius of such a foundation.

The constitution of authority in legislature follows in importance the constitution of law; for authority is the living guardian of the dead text of law. Now, what was the constitution of authority among the Hebrews? It has been often said, if I mistake not, that it was theocratic; this is an error. From the earliest times, Moses and Aaron divided the power; one was the military and civil chief, the other the religious chief, and that distinction between the temporal and spiritual order—deeply traced by the double memorial of the legislator and the pontiff—continues throughout the whole history of the Jewish people, notwithstanding the accidental gathering of the whole authority in one and the same hand. If the pontificate and the supreme judicature blend together in Samuel, they become separated in the times of David and the kings; if they are found united after the captivity, they separated again before Jesus Christ. The Hebraic community, like the Catholic community, was based upon the distinction between the spiritual and the temporal powers, a distinction without which a nation would neither be able to preserve truth nor liberty. Truth, because being of a higher order, it could not keep its place under a sceptre transmitted by purely human means; liberty, because all the social and regular forces, being concentred under the sceptre of one single mind and one single action, it becomes impossible for any one to defend his feeble personality against the omnipotent personality of the State. The people, crushed under the weight of such a formidable unity, would doubtless writhe like the giant under the weight of Etna; but their force, not being united under a stable and recognized organization, their efforts would result only in futile shocks, by which, if they succeeded in overthrowing the order that weighed upon them, their very victory would still cost them their liberty, for to destroy order is also to destroy liberty. By the division of power into two branches, not opposed to each other—not even rivals, so much do their attributes differ—opinion obtains a pacific support against force, right against oppression, and society, notwithstanding its vicissitudes, being united without violence, duly performs its office for time and for eternity.

However, this admirable order has nowhere been able to establish itself, save among the Jewish people and in nations entirely Christian, that is to say, Catholic. Everywhere else, the State has not failed to absorb the whole of human nature in its rapacious unity. And this, gentlemen, should not excite our wonder: the spiritual power, being by its very essence a disarmed power, God alone is able to communicate to it the inner force which it needs peacefully to resist the temporal power. Where God is not, intrigue, baseness, fear, soon bend mind to matter; and the spiritual order, should it still exist, remains but a miserable phantom, to which the State leaves a reed for sceptre, contempt for protection, and a little gold for pay. Inasmuch, then, as the Jewish people, as well as the Catholic nations, possessed the prerogative of a true spiritual power, it is stamped with a character of pre-eminence, which no other people can dispute with it in the times anterior to Christ.

The constitution of family was not less remarkable in the Jewish people than the constitution of law and authority. The individuals whose union forms families, and whom we may call domestic individuals, namely, the father, the mother, the child, and the servant, stood there in relations full of order and equity. Moses, it is true, did not formally substitute the unity of the conjugal tie in place of eastern polygamy; but he instilled the practice of it by establishing the faculty of repudiation for certain cases, by forbidding the future kings of Israel to have a great number of wives, like the princes of the East, and in supposing but once only in his whole legislation that a man may have two wives. Thus, save a few examples noticed in the course of Scripture, the Hebraic family appears to us, under this head, in a state analogous to that of the Christian family. The unity of marriage was a custom among them. The authority of the father over the child was great, without extending to that right over life and death which too often made an executioner's office of paternity among the ancients. The servant belonged to the family by virtue of a voluntary agreement; no Hebrew could be the slave of another Hebrew; and even engagements for perpetual service were permitted by law only after a trial of seven years. The stranger alone, by right of conquest, was liable to slavery, properly so called; and even this bondage, kept within certain limits, was far from producing that contempt and that abuse of man which we remark among the peoples anterior to Jesus Christ. All the Jewish families were ranged in twelve tribes, corresponding to the twelve patriarchs, sons of Jacob, and forming of the nation twelve great families, united in the bond of the same blood, and so much the more strongly, as it flowed from the same father by twelve perfectly recognizable sources. Nothing in antiquity is comparable to this constitution of the Hebraic family.

It is the same in regard to the bases upon which the system of proprietorship rested among them. Houses and lands could only be alienated for a lapse of forty-nine years. After that, they returned to their former possessor or to his heirs. The object of this singular arrangement was to prevent the ruin of families and the too great inequality of fortunes, without hindering, however, the necessary movement of commerce and industry. The rich man bought of the unfortunate or erring man the whole or a part of his patrimony, and enjoyed possession of it for half a century; but the son or grandson of the despoiled proprietor cherished in his heart the hope of returning again to the roof of his ancestors. By a second and no less remarkable regulation, the fields could not be cultivated more than six years in seven; they rested the seventh year, and all the fruit which they bore naturally in a land covered with vines and olive-trees belonged to the poor, as their share in the common patrimony of Israel.

Such was, in the most fundamental matters, that celebrated legislation of Moses, the invulnerable stability of which time has respected, and which has placed that great man at the head of all those who have had the rare distinction of giving laws to nations.

But legislation is only the first element of the

life of a people; art is the second. Legislation classes a people in the order of acts, art determines its rank in the order of ideas and of their expression. The greater the idea the greater is the visible monument it raises up, and which causes it to subsist even after it has perished in the mind that conceived it. Now the monument of Hebraic ideas is a book which forms part of the book of books, a book which forms the preface to the Gospel, and which in that illustrious vicinity obtains respect as the finished pedestal of a faultless statue. As history, the Hebrew Bible precedes all histories by its antiquity, continuity, and authenticity; alone it mounts to the cradle of the human race, and lays down the first stone of the whole edifice of the past. As a juridical compilation, it is without equal in any of the collections containing the laws of great communities. As moral philosophy, it opposes its books of wisdom to all the maxims of the most renowned sages, and a presence of God is felt in them which elevates the soul above the natural reach of reason. As poesy, it contains the hymns of David and the prophets, repeated after two or three thousand years by all the echoes of the Christian world, and become creators of a language which has passed into all human tongues for lauding and blessing God. Other peoples have had historians, jurisconsults, sages, poets, but which are their own, and form, as it were, a separate glory; the Jewish people has been the historian, the jurisconsult, the sage, the poet of mankind.

Its territory also answered to that great place which we behold it occupying. For the support and nourishment of its body, it had received a land equally illustrious with its legislation and its art. Cast a glance upon a map of the world, and you will quickly perceive there a point which forms the centre of Asia, Africa, and Europe; which, washed by the waves of the Mediterranean, touches by them those healthy and genial climates where in the plenitude of human activity the hardy race of Japhet exercises its energy; whilst, on another hand, the River Euphrates and the Gulf of the Red Sea open to its inhabitants the routes of the Indian Ocean, permitting them to seek under the equatorial zones those fabulous riches which Solomon explored, which Alexander desired to see, which the Romans coveted, which the Middle Ages discovered anew, which the British power now guards with such supreme jealousy. In close vicinity also to that favored point of the globe, you will perceive Memphis, the Nile, the Pyramids, and those sublime deserts which to the present time have rebelled against the most courageous curiosity, so that its boundaries having gates open to all, had them also closed against all. There, as at an inevitable rendezvous indicated by nature and God, all the conquerors have appeared. The primitive monarchies of Assur and Chaldæa unceasingly sent there their generals. Alexander was halted there before Tyre, and went to read in Jerusalem the history of his triumphs written beforehand, like those of Cyrus; his successors contested desperately for this remnant of his crown; the Romans took possession of it; all the chivalry of the Middle Ages pressed there during two hundred years; Napoleon caused a gleam of his sword to shine upon its sands; in fine, but yesterday the last thunder of European cannon awakened the old echoes of that proud land; and the discerning finger of those who observe the future points to it as the future battle-ground for the combats reserved to our descendants. You have named Syria, gentlemen, and with it the territory given to the Jewish people as the temporal complement of those magnificent graces which they had received in the mental order.

Nevertheless, gentlemen, a people is not yet fully known when we know its territory, its art, and its legislation; it is necessary also to know its history. The history of a people is the course of its acts for the preservation of its laws, ideas, customs, territory, all, in fine, that constitutes its proper life and civilization. The more magnificent its endowments the more is it accountable towards God and man for the devotedness shown by it in defence of the gifts which are not only its personal patrimony, but which form part of the general dotation of mankind, and enter into the plans by which Providence conducts all things to their end. And, according as a people acquits itself well or ill of this great task, it marks in history its degree of shame or renown. What, gentlemen, has formed the dignity of our history? It is that having received from God a territory which is the heart of Europe, we have held it under faithful guardianship for fourteen hundred years, permitting none but ourselves to settle between the Alps and the Pyrenees; it is that having among all the barbarous nations received the firstfruits of the Catholic faith, we have preserved it to the end, neither permitting this, the elder kingdom of Christendom, to be entirely corrupted by heresy nor overcome by doubt; it is that having received, in fine, the most ancient and the most free monarchy of Europe, we have preserved in a happy balance, although it has been often troubled, the double spirit of authority and liberty, being equally incapable of supporting anarchy or absolute power. We have, in a word, preserved in the body of Europe a land of faith, order, and liberty.

The Jewish people had yet greater duties, and a more perilous position imposed upon it. Feeble in number, and cast upon a part of the world which by its position tempted all the neighboring empires, it had to protect against them, with its independence, laws and traditions upon which the destinies of the world depended. No people entrusted with a more precious charge, in more favorable conditions, has shown such remarkable and persevering magnanimity in defending it. Not to see this would be an act of blindness, not to acknowledge it an act of ingratitude. Nineveh, Babylon, Memphis, by turns, and sometimes together, conspired for the destruction of that handful of Israelites; innumerable armies, led by powerful kings, invaded their territory, and laid siege to their capital; often victorious, they often purchased their glory at the cost of cruel reverses. Ten of their tribes, carried into captivity, have disappeared from history: the two others afterwards followed the same road of exile from whence nations never return. But seventy years of adversity far from their country did not weary the hearts of the captives; by science and beauty they penetrated into the palaces of kings, and governed their conquerors. Cyrus delivers them, Alexander visits them, and when, in the heart of Asia, a new and a more terrible persecution brings into their temple the desolation of impiety, they raise up in their midst, to save their country and religion, that race of the Maccabees whose name has become for peoples oppressed by stronger than themselves the very name of courage and right. And this heroic spectacle, gentlemen, lasted fifteen hundred years! For fifteen hundred consecutive years Israel held her place against the great empires of the world; and when at length Rome had surmounted all and subjected all, when the whole earth had kept silence before her for more than a century, Israel still struggled in the mountains and valleys of Judæa for the remnants of her liberty. Rome was forced to send her legions and her captains against such memorable perseverance, and Jerusalem, yet once more besieged, sent up to heaven, in an implacable defence, the last generous cry which the Romans were destined to hear.

Was it ended, gentlemen? Did not this people, without territory and without princes, wander to die in obscurity upon the vast surface over which the still timid will of their conquerors had scattered it? For any other, indeed, the hour of death would have come. But the Israelites remembered the days of their captivity, when they hung their harps upon the willows of Babylon, because they could not sing the songs of Sion in a strange land; as they had then carried their laws and traditions with them to be their eternal principle of life, they again bore them over the whole earth. They demanded their subsistence from labor, their dignity from the memorials of their ancestors, their consolation from the God who had brought them out of Egypt by Moses, out of Chaldæa by Cyrus, and who was able, when he willed, to bring them back again to that Jerusalem already raised from its ruins, and become the object of the combats of all Christendom. This people, whom their founder called a hard people, and who in fact opposed to adversity a soul of granite, this people still lives—lives everywhere. Disinherited from their country, the children of Israel have sought in commerce that moveable wealth which may be hidden more quickly than persecution advances; and we now see kings tributaries to their activity, unblushingly recurring to the venerated purse of some Hebrew for the accomplishment of their designs and the aggrandisement of their glory. Yet once more, Israel lives; she has lived for seventeen centuries without chief, without temple, without territory, often persecuted, but preserving, as in Jerusalem, her antique and immoveable ideas, and having in addition that unique glory of subsisting from an inner force sustained by nothing from without, and which nourishes itself at the mysterious altar of a superhuman past. Do you not see that she defies you? That alone among nations she counts four thousand years of duration? That nothing prognosticates the end of such a scandal against the nature of things? Dig out her tomb if you can; set your surest seal upon it; place your guards around it: she will but laugh at you and rise again, proving to you yet once more that she lives of a spirit which you have not, and that matter can do nought against spirit.

I have the right to conclude, gentlemen, that the Jewish people, under the social point of view, is the most important monument of the times anterior to Christ. It is not less so under the religious point of view; and here I shall need but very short observations.

For, remark that whilst all nations were plunged in the darkness of idolatry, Greeks, Romans, Assyrians, Egyptians, that little people adored one only God; and antiquity spake with wonder of the empty temple of Jerusalem, because it did not see God represented there by any image capable of impressing the senses—not that such representation is an evil in itself, as long as it does not touch the true character of the Divinity; but the Hebrews had such a horror of idols that they preferred, according to the order of their legislator, to leave God in their temple in his total invisibility rather than expose their faith to the impressive charm of some striking representation. For idolatry not only attacked them from without, it seized upon their heart, and they often fell before it. But, notwithstanding this double temptation, they never failed to return to that God of their fathers of whom they were the sole adorers.

By the dogma of creation they had an idea of

him which always completely separated them from idolaters. These rendered no account to themselves of the existence of the universe, or if they sought to penetrate its secret, they willingly believed it to be contemporary with their gods, giving to them at most some secondary action upon universal substance. The Jews had quite another doctrine, expressed from the first sign of their sacred Scriptures by that astounding phrase: "In the beginning God created the heavens and the earth."[1] Had they possessed but that single doctrinal expression, they would have been richer in knowledge of God than all the schools and all the religions of antiquity. In a word, the Jewish people was the only people before Jesus Christ which had a clear notion of the Divinity, and which rendered to him a worship free from the puerile dreams of the imagination and the taint of shameless sensuality. I may then conclude that in the religious, as in the social point of view, the Hebrew nation was the most important monument of the times anterior to Jesus Christ.

I add that Jesus Christ was the soul of that nation, and pre-existed in it by a life which we are about to verify.

---

[1] Gen. i. 1.

I ought to have grown weary, gentlemen, of pointing out to you the peculiarities of the Jews. There is one, however, which surpasses all the rest, and of which I have as yet said nothing. I mean the Messianic idea which circulated in their veins as their purest blood, and without which it is impossible to explain either their faith or their destinies. The Messianic idea is composed of four elements. Under its influence, the Jews believed, in the first place, that the one God and Creator adored by them would some day become the God of the whole earth. In addition, they believed that that revolution would be brought about by a single man called the Messiah, the Holy One, the Just, the Saviour, the Desired of nations. They believed that this man would be a Jew of the tribe of Judah and of the house of David. They believed, in fine, that this predestinated man would suffer and die in order to accomplish the work of transformation with which Providence had charged him.

That such was their faith it is easy for us to learn even of themselves, since they still live, and since, notwithstanding four thousand years of expectation which, in their eyes, has not been realized, they have never ceased to render unshaken testimony to the hopes of their ancestors. But, gentlemen, let us not be content with their present testimony; let us open the monuments of their history, and follow the progress of the Messianic idea through the principal phases that mark the development of the nation itself, such as its birth, its formation into a people, the point of its maturity, its decadency, its captivity, and its restoration at the foot of the second temple, raised up by Zorababel.

Behold us in the fields of Chaldæa with Abraham; we are about to hear the first words, which formed, as it were, the seed of the Hebrew race. Observe, gentlemen, that we are not now examining whether these words are true, whether they were from God; we have now simply to show the idea which the Jewish people had of themselves, and of their mission here below. Whether they deceived themselves in this idea is another question, to be judged afterwards.

God, then, according to the Hebrew monuments, says to Abraham: "Go forth out of thy country, and from thy kindred, and out of thy father's house, and come into the land which I will show thee; and I will make of thee a great nation, and I will bless thee, and magnify thy name, and thou shalt be blessed. I will bless them that bless thee, and curse them that curse thee, and in thee shall all the kindred of the earth be blessed."[1] Thus, at the same moment, and in an inseparable manner, two thousand years before Jesus Christ, the Jewish people appeared in the world, and therewith the Messianic idea—the idea that Israel was the depositary of a blessing which was to spread over the whole universe.

Abraham goes forth from Chaldæa, and settles in the land promised to his posterity. He waits there even to an advanced old age for the son to whom he is to transmit the Messianic heritage; that son is given to him; and when the child has attained all the graces of youth, God calls upon the patriarch to offer him in sacrifice upon a mysterious mountain. With unshaken faith in the wisdom and goodness of God, the old man raises his hand upon his only and well-beloved son, and he hears that second declaration, stronger and more distinct than the first: "By my own self have I sworn, saith the Lord, because thou hast done this thing, and hast not spared thy only-begotten son for my sake; I will

---

[1] Gen. xii. 1-3.

bless thee, and I will multiply thy seed as the stars of heaven, and as the sand that is by the sea shore: thy seed shall possess the gates of their enemies, and in thy seed shall all the nations of the earth be blessed." [1] An oath is added to the force of the promise; and it is more clearly indicated that the Messianic benediction should spread over the whole human race, not by Abraham himself, but by his posterity.

Isaac, the son of Abraham, hears the same promise and the same prophecy: they are repeated to Jacob, the son of Isaac. The three first Hebrew generations, thus confirmed in the hope of the Messiah, spread out in twelve patriarchs, fathers of twelve tribes; and Jacob, about to die, assembles them around his bed to close the first Messianic age by a solemn prophecy, which sums up the preceding ones, giving, at the same time, additional precision to them. Surrounded then, by his twelve children, he announces to each of them, by some characteristic traits, what will be his lot in the future. Having arrived at Judah, he says these memorable words to him: "Judah, thee shall thy brethren praise: thy hands shall

---

[1] Gen. xxii. 16–18.

be on the necks of thy enemies; the sons of thy father shall bow down to thee. Judah is a lion's whelp: to the prey, my son, thou art gone up; resting thou hast couched as a lion, and as a lioness: who shall rouse him? The sceptre shall not be taken away from Judah, nor a ruler from his thigh, till he come that is to be sent, and he shall be the expectation of nations."[1] Thus, at the moment when the patriarchal inheritance becomes subdivided into twelve branches, the branch from which the Messiah is to be born is designated; it is to be that of Judah; and the day predestined for the appearance of the Messiah is marked by a sign which posterity will easily recognize.

The blood of Abraham, Isaac, and Jacob is henceforth fertile; it multiplies in a land which has given it hospitality; and having soon become an object of fear and jealousy, it passes from exile to bondage, in order to serve in tribulation an apprenticeship necessary to its high destinies. Its enemies think to destroy, they do but strengthen it. The Israelites are a people. Moses brings them out of Egypt, and leads them across the desert to the foot of Sinai, from whence

---

[1] Gen. xlix. 8–10.

come the laws which are to govern them. Follow, gentlemen, follow that marvellous march of so great a people; the eyes of your childhood formerly gazed upon its wonders, look at them again with the thought of riper years. From encampment to encampment the children of Israel arrive before Jordan, to the frontiers of that territory inhabited by their first ancestors, and the possession of which is promised to their posterity. There they meet a whole people in arms awaiting those adventurers who despoiled Egypt, and whose march has resounded from the desert even to the hills of Judæa. Moab has ranged her battalions, she has raised her altars, convoked her chiefs; the children of Israel are afoot, with their wives, their children, their soldiers, their Levites, bearing, hidden under the skins of animals, the tabernacle of the God who has just spoken to them from Sinai. A man of the East advances between the two peoples. "Balac," says he, "Balac, king of the Moabites, hath brought me from Aram, from the mountains of the east: Come, said he, and curse Jacob; make haste and detest Israel. How shall I curse him whom God hath not cursed? By what means shall I detest him whom the Lord detesteth not? I shall see him from the top of the rocks, and shall consider him from the hills. This people shall dwell alone, and shall not be reckoned among the nations. Who can count the dust of Jacob, and know the number of the stock of Israel?"[1] These unexpected blessings alarm Moab; the prophet is implored to change his language; if he will not curse, they pray him at least not to bless. Thrice Balaam opens his mouth; thrice he blesses the conquering people before him; and at last the Messianic prophecy escapes from him as in spite of himself: "I shall see him, but not now: I shall behold him, but not near. A star shall rise out of Jacob, and a sceptre shall spring up from Israel, and shall strike the chiefs of Moab, and shall waste the children of Seth. . . . Alas! who shall live when God shall do these things? They shall come in galleys from Italy, they shall overcome the Assyrians, and shall waste the Hebrews, and at last they themselves also shall perish."[2]

Observe again, gentlemen, that we are not now examining whether Balaam was or was not a prophet, but simply showing the course of the Messianic idea in the historical life of the Jewish

---

[1] Numb. xxiii. 7-10.   [2] Ibid. xxiv. 17, 23, 24.

people. You see this idea taking here a new development; it is no longer a patriarch of Israel who announces the coming of the Messiah, and the establishment of his reign over all the children of Seth, that is to say of Adam, but a stranger. And he marks the circumstances of his coming with most strange perspicacity, since he even designates the domination of the Romans over the East and over the Jewish people as the precursory sign of the Messiah's appearance.

David and Solomon mark the highest point of the Hebrew monarchy, and with them commence the national and religious hymns known by the name of psalms. Sung in the temple of Jerusalem on the great feast days, they publicly expressed the inner feeling, the hopes and desires of the whole nation. Now it is easy to recognize here the Messianic idea disclosing itself on all occasions in the soul of poet and people. On reading them you will remark passages such as this: "All the ends of the earth shall remember and shall be converted to the Lord: and all the kindreds of the Gentiles shall adore in his sight, for the kingdom is the Lord's; and he shall have dominion over the nations. All the fat ones of the earth have eaten, and have adored: all they that go down to the earth shall fall before him."[1]

Later also, at the approach of the decadency and captivity — seven hundred years, however, before Jesus Christ — the Messianic idea assumed in Isaiah a clearness and an abundance of expression which it is impossible to render to you, since I should weary you by the number and length of the passages I should have to cite. It is he who sees the Messiah springing from the race of Jesse, the father of David, and who at the same time describes, as if from Calvary or the Vatican, the glory of the sufferings and triumphs of Jesus Christ. "Arise, arise, put on thy strength, O Sion; put on the garments of thy glory, O Jerusalem, the city of the holy One: for henceforth the uncircumcised and unclean shall no more pass through thee."[2] "How beautiful upon the mountains are the feet of him that bringeth good tidings, and that preacheth peace: of him that showeth forth good, that preacheth salvation, that saith to Sion: Thy God shall reign!"[3] "The Lord hath prepared his holy arm in the sight of all the Gentiles, and all the ends of the earth shall see the salvation of our God."[4] "Behold

---

[1] Ps. xxi. 28-30.   [2] Is. lii. 1.   [3] Ibid. 7.   [4] Ibid. 10.

my servant shall understand, he shall be exalted and extolled, and he shall be exceeding high. As many have been astonished at thee so shall his visage be inglorious among men, and his form among the sons of men. He shall sprinkle many nations. Kings shall shut their mouth at him: for they to whom it was not told of him have seen, and they that heard not have beheld."[1] And immediately after, Isaiah begins the description of the sufferings and ignominies of Calvary, which he completes in twelve consecutive verses. Then he continues resuming his hymns of triumph: "He that hath made thee shall rule over thee, the Lord of hosts is his name; and thy Redeemer, the holy One of Israel, shall be called the God of all the earth."[2]

But it is at Babylon, during the captivity, six hundred years before Jesus Christ, that the Messianic idea becomes invested with a form which attains to mathematical clearness and precision. Must I recall to you the prophecy of Daniel? Listen then to it: "Seventy weeks are shortened upon thy people, and upon the holy city, that transgression may be finished, and sin may have an end, and everlasting justice may be

---

[1] Is. lii. 13–15.   [2] Ibid. liv. 5.

brought, and vision and prophecy may be fulfilled, and the Saint of saints be anointed. Know thou therefore and take notice that from the going forth of the word to build up Jerusalem again unto Christ the Prince, there shall be seven weeks and sixty-two weeks: and the street shall be built again, and the walls in the straitness of times. And after sixty-two weeks Christ shall be slain: and the people that shall deny him shall not be his. And a people with their leader that shall come shall destroy the city and the sanctuary: and the end thereof shall be waste, and after the end of the war the appointed desolation. And he shall confirm the covenant with many, in one week: and in the half of the week the victim and the sacrifice shall fail: and there shall be in the temple the abomination of desolation: and the desolation shall continue even to the consummation, and to the end."[1]

I do not stop, gentlemen, to examine the striking features of this discourse, which resembles less a vision of the future than a narration of the past. The course of my subject bears me on and brings me to the foot of the second temple, to hear, five hundred years before Jesus Christ, those last

---
[1] Dan. ix. 24-27.

words of the prophet Aggeus: "Yet one little while, and I will move the heaven, and the earth, and the sea, and the dry land, and I will move all nations: and the Desired of all nations shall come: and I will fill this house with glory, saith the Lord of hosts. . . . Great shall be the glory of this last house more than of the first, and in this place will I give peace."[1]

What continuity, gentlemen, through so many eventful centuries! What fidelity to one and the same idea from so many men separated by ages! But the Messianic idea was not even confined to the special tradition of the Jewish people; it passed over Jordan, the Euphrates, the Indus, the Mediterranean, all the oceans, and, borne upon the invisible wings of Providence, it penetrated all the most diverse and most distant nations, to create among them a uniform hope and a universal remembrance. Confucius, at the eastern extremity of Asia, spoke of a saint who, he said, was the *true saint*, and who would appear in the West. Virgil, translating into verse the oracles of the Cumæan Sibyl, announced to the Augustan age the coming of a mysterious child, a son of Jupiter, destined to banish from the world the

---

Aggeus ii. 7-10.

vestiges of iniquity, and to commence an order of things as great as new. Tacitus, on the reign of Vespasian, thus expresses himself: "It was a widely-spread belief that, according to ancient sacerdotal writings, at that very epoch, the East should prevail, and that men come from Judæa should seize the government of things." The rationalists of the eighteenth century, constrained by evidence, have often avowed that unanimity of the Messianic expectation. Voltaire said: "From time immemorial it was a maxim among the Indians and the Chinese that the sage would come from the West; Europe, on the contrary, declared that the sage would come from the East."[1] Volney said: "The sacred and mythological traditions of former times had spread throughout Asia the belief in a great mediator who was to come, a final judge, a future saviour, king, God, conqueror and legislator, who would bring back again the golden age upon earth and deliver men from the empire of evil."[2] Boulanger, under a still more general form, confessed that all nations held "an expectation of that nature;" and he adds this astounding phrase: that

---

[1] " Additions a l' Histoire Generale," page 15.
[2] " Les Ruines," page 228.

the East may be said to be "the pole of the hope of all nations"[1] It is the very saying of Jacob on his death-bed.

It is then certain, gentlemen, that the Messianic idea was the life of the Jewish people during the course of the two thousand years which preceded Jesus Christ, and that idea was held among all the nations of the earth with such unanimity, that it is not even possible to account for it by the communications of the Hebrews with the Gentiles, but it is necessary to suppose a diffusion of that idea even anterior to Abraham. And that Messianic idea, so extraordinary in its universality, its progress, its perseverance, and its precision, is it at length fulfilled? Yes, it is fulfilled; the one God, creator of the Hebraic Bible, has become the God of nearly all the earth; and the very nations that have not yet accepted him render homage to him by a certain number of adorers whom Providence elects from their midst. And who has accomplished this incredible revolution? One single man, Christ. And whence came this man, Christ? He was a Jew, of the tribe of Judah, of the house of David. And how has he accomplished this prodigious social and religious

---

[1] "Recherches sur l' Origine du Despotisme oriental," section x.

revolution? By suffering and dying, as David, Isaiah, Daniel, had foretold.

And now, gentlemen, what think you of it? Here are two parallel and corresponding facts, both certain, both of colossal proportion, one which lasted two thousand years before Jesus Christ, the other which has lasted eighteen hundred years since Jesus Christ; one which announces a great revolution, and a revolution impossible to foresee, the other which is its accomplishment, both having Jesus Christ for principle, for end, and for bond of union. Yet once more, what think you of it? Are you bold enough to deny it? But what would you deny? The existence of the Messianic idea? It is in the Jewish people, still living, in all the continuous monuments of its history, in the universal traditions of the human race, in the most positive avowals of the most profound unbelief. Would you deny the anteriority of the prophetic details? The Jews, who crucified Jesus Christ, and who have a national and traditional interest in depriving him of the proofs of his divinity, declare to you that their Scriptures were formerly what they are now, and for additional certainty, two hundred and fifty years before Jesus Christ, under Ptolemy

Philadelphus, king of Egypt, all the Old Testament, translated into Greek, fell into the possession of the Greek world, the Roman world, and the whole civilized world. Would you turn to the other pole of the question, and deny the accomplishment of the Messianic idea? The Catholic Church, the offspring of that idea, is before your eyes—she has baptized you. Would you stand upon the point of junction of those two formidable events? Would you deny that Jesus Christ has verified the Messianic idea in his person, that he was a Jew, of the tribe of Judah, of the house of David, and the founder of the Catholic Church upon the double ruin of the synagogue and idolatry? The two interested parties—and they are irreconcilable enemies—confess all this. The Jew affirms it, and the Christian affirms it. Would you say that this juncture of colossal events at the precise point of Jesus Christ is the result of chance? Were it even so, chance is but a brief and fortuitous accident—its definition excludes the idea of continuity; there is no chance of two thousand years' duration and of eighteen centuries added thereto. In fine, would you say that it is the result of a long conspiracy, by which the ambitious and theological Jewish people sought to create for itself a great existence? What! a conspiracy lasting two thousand years founded upon a chief whom sixty generations had to wait for, and whom it was necessary to create after having so patiently waited for him! Alas! it is no easy matter to conspire in favor of a living man; what must it be to conspire in favor of a man who does not exist, and who, it is supposed, will be born at an indefinite epoch! And remark that when that man came, the Jews crucified him—doubtless because his crucifixion formed part of the conspiracy. Observe also that they denied him after as well as before the crucifixion —doubtless in order to secure the final success of the conspiracy and all the success of ambition and theology which they expected therefrom!

Gentlemen, when God works there is nothing to be done against him. The proportions of the work of Christ in the times which preceded him are yet more striking than all the divine proportions of his life and his after-life. For, in fine, when a man lives, he is a power, he has an action; it is possible to conceive that certain circumstances may have favored a man of rare genius, and have given him great ascendancy over his contemporaries Even after death there remain friends, disciples, the remembrance of an existence which was real, and consequently a surviving means of action. But what are we able to do upon that which precedes us, upon the past? Who among us, however eminent he may be, is able to make an ancestor for himself? Who among us, desiring to found a doctrine, is able to create for himself an avant-garde of generations already faithful to a teaching which had not yet been heard? Who among us will present his doctrinal ancestry to the world, if he be not truly the son of a doctrine anterior to himself? Ah! the past is a land closed against us; the past is not even a place wherein God can act, unless he act there beforehand and by way of preparation. Had Jesus Christ been like one of us, fallen without a providential pre-existence between the past and the future, he would in vain have demanded from history accomplished and closed a pedestal which would bear him back twenty centuries beyond his cradle. Instead of this, Abraham, Isaac, Jacob, David, Isaiah, Jeremiah, Ezekiel, Daniel, a whole people, the human race itself, came to meet and salute him in the arms of the aged Simeon, exclaiming in the name of all the past, of which he is the last representative: "Now lettest thou thy servant depart, O Lord, according to thy word, in peace. Because mine eyes have seen thy salvation, which thou hast prepared before the face of all people: a light to lighten the Gentiles, and the glory of thy people Israel."[1]

We have reached the summit, gentlemen; Jesus Christ appears before us as the moving principle of the past as well as of the future, the soul of the times which preceded him as well as of the times which follow him. He appears before us in his ancestry, upheld by the Jewish people, the most important social and religious monument of ancient times; and in his posterity, upheld by the Catholic Church, the greatest social and religious work of modern times. He appears before us, holding in his left hand the Old Testament, the greatest book of the times which preceded him, and in his right hand the Gospel, the greatest book of the times which come after him. And yet, so preceded, and so followed, he is still greater in himself than his ancestors and his posterity, than the patriarchs and the prophets, than the apostles and the martyrs. Supported by all that is most illustrious before and

---

[1] St. Luke ii. 29-32.

after him, his personal physiognomy still stands out from this sublime scene, and, by outshining that which seemed above all, reveals to us the God who has neither model nor equal. Therefore, in presence of this triple sign of divinity—before, during, and after—in ancestry, in posterity, and even during life, let us stand up, gentlemen, let us all stand up together, whoever we may be, believers and unbelievers. Let us stand up, believers, with feelings of respect, admiration, faith, love, for a God who has revealed himself to us with so much evidence, and who has chosen us among men to be the depositaries of that splendid manifestation of his truth! And you who do not believe stand up also, but with fear and trembling, as men who are but as nothing with their power and their reasoning, before facts which fill all ages, and which are in themselves so full of the power and majesty of God!

THE EFFORTS OF RATIONALISM TO DESTROY THE LIFE OF JESUS CHRIST.

My Lord—Gentlemen,

Jesus Christ lived as God, he has outlived himself as God, he pre-existed as God; he pre-existed in the Jewish people, he has expressed his life in the Gospel, he has outlived that life in the Church; and it is this triple circle of his manifestation that has rendered his divinity triumphant here below. As soon as the human race possessed full consciousness of this, it became, so to say, overwhelmed by such a demonstration, and from Theodosius to Louis XIV.—for the space of thirteen hundred years—discussion seemed impossible against Christ—in this sense at least, that all yielded to him, or accepted him as their foundation. But, this time having passed, rationalism, which had been dethroned by Jesus Christ, attempted to claim again the empire it had lost; it thought that, as ages had covered all that formidable edifice with their billows, some chances were possible in favor of doubt and negation, and that the eighteenth century of the Christian era could be called upon to render willing reprisals and new judgments against a doctrine grown old by time. Rationalism thus found itself again in presence of Jesus Christ, standing himself between the Catholic Church and the Jewish people, as between the right and left wings of truth; and a triple war was planned, in order to overthrow the work whose building up was in past times accomplished in spite of the powerless efforts which were now to be renewed. The Jewish people was described as a vile, an ignoble, an odious race, unworthy of any credit or respect; the Catholic Church as an instrument of misery for the people, of bondage for the intelligence, of subjection for nations and kings. I have defended the Church before you, gentlemen, for many long years; yesterday, I restored the true physiognomy of the Jewish people; I shall not return to either of these during these discussions. Jesus Christ calls me to-day into the very heart of the combat of which he is the object and the chief. The Jewish people was composed of men, and so is also the Catholic Church; and, however great men may be, they are not altogether exempt, even when bearing in their hearts the Spirit of God, from some failing and some infirmity; it is not so with Christ. Miraculous in his perfection, he does not suffer, as the Gospel shows him, any human doubt; and if he really stands upon that faultless pedestal, it is vain for rationalism to fulminate, on the right hand and on the left, its powerless thunder against him. Christ, impassible in the centre of Catholic truth, shelters all under his impregnable divinity. It was, then, necessary to destroy Jesus Christ, either by annihilating his life, by perverting it, or at least by explaining it away. This has been attempted, gentlemen; and the exposition of this triple effort will terminate our conferences for this year. Let us commence with the most decisive of the three —that which had for its object the annihilation of the life of Christ.

Is Christ a chimera or a reality? Does he belong to fable or to history? This is the question. It may astonish you, gentlemen, and yet it is serious; for clever men have boldly denied the existence of Jesus Christ; and others, without venturing to this extreme audacity, have sought at least to weaken the certainty of his life, and artfully to lessen its historical splendor. It becomes necessary, then, to place, or rather to maintain,

Jesus Christ in history; and to this end we must first of all learn the nature and the laws of history; for as long as we are unacquainted with them, it will be impossible for us to decide whether Jesus Christ is or is not a historical personage. I proceed, then, to treat of history; we shall afterwards see whether Christ is present in it or absent from it.

Man lives in time, that is to say, in a singular element, which causes him at the same time to live and to die; he advances between a past which is no more and a future yet to come; and if he did not possess the faculty of concentrating in himself these three states of his existence, he would be but incessantly coming into the world without ever attaining to the possession of life. For hardly would he have made a step in advance before forgetfulness would have obliterated its traces, and thus he would be constantly before himself like a vapor rising from the earth and vanishing away. Against this terrible power of time, God has given him memory, by which man lives in the past as well as in the present; so that resuscitating his ancient days at pleasure, he beholds himself in the plenitude of his personality, like an edifice whose stones have been placed successively but which the eye surveys and perceives entire. Now the memory that suffices for the life of a single man is not sufficient for mankind; whilst man is one, with a memory subsisting as long as himself, mankind is multiple, and its memory expires with each generation, or at most but little of it is transmitted to the future generation. The father tells the son what he has seen, the son relates it to the grandson, but at each stage remembrance grows more obscure, and little by little the light of that tradition brightens only the distant heights of the most important events. It ends, however, by becoming defaced; its lines grow confused to the eyes of a posterity continually retreating before them; and if God did not intervene to bring help to the human race losing all traces of itself, we should be living in an eternal state of infancy, between a past about which we are untaught and a future entirely unknown to us. Experience, the source of all progress, would constantly be wanting. Neither truth nor error, neither good nor evil would be known, save by a puerile combat recommencing always at the same point—a spectacle unworthy of man, unworthy of God—where truth and good, having no adequate field of action, would never be able to display their characters of stability and immortality. God, who, by memory, had provided for the progressive identity of man, should evidently have provided also for the continuous perpetuity of the human race by a memory conformable to the destinies of this vast body, that is to say, by a united, a universal, a certain memory, capable of giving to mankind complete consciousness of its works from the beginning to the end. In so speaking, gentlemen, I have defined history.

History is the life of mankind present to itself, as our life is present to us; history is the memory of the world. But what difficulties lie in the way of its formation! God lights a torch in our intelligence which enlightens our past, because he is our intelligence itself, one and indivisible; but how is the human race, multiple and divided, to be endowed with a similar light? How is an immortal memory to be given to the human race which dies daily? An immutable memory to that which is but change? A certain memory to that which doubts so easily about all that it does not see? God provided for this in giving us writing. By means of writing, a thing once said may be always heard, a spectacle once witnessed may be always visible; writing seizes the passing wave and renders it eternal. This is already immortality and immutability, but it is not yet certainty. For the false can be written as well as the true. A thing may indeed be written, but who will guarantee its truth to us? A man two thousand years ago writes a book, wherein he relates things which he says he witnessed: who will prove to us that he speaks the truth, and that a fable has not reached us under the seeming garb of history? Evidently, writing alone does not answer to this question; history begins with it, but it is not history in all its elements. History, if there be any, should command our minds with the same authority as the other powers which have received a mission to govern them. As there is a moral force in the world which does not permit us to say it is lawful for the child to kill his father, a mathematical force which does not permit us to build a house upon a plan without equilibrium, so also there should exist in the world a historical force which would not permit us to say to history: Thou hast spoken falsely. If this force exist not, there is no history.

What are, then, the conditions of history; or

rather what are the conditions of a historical writing? For writing is the fundamental, persisting, substantial element of history. Without writing, there remains to us nothing but tradition more or less confused; but as writing may deceive, it is needful that we should know the conditions which elevate writing to the state of historical writing, that is to say, to the state of authentic, certain, infallible, true writing. These conditions are three in number.

In the first place, writing must be public. All that is secret is without authority; every mysterious document is valueless because it has not been verified. Nothing of this is powerful but by public verification. The people form the only notary capable of certifying their own history, because they form the assemblage of all ages, of all ideas, of all interests, and because a popular conspiracy formed to lie to posterity is even impossible to conceive. A man fabricates error; a people has too many diverse ideas and passions to be able to combine together to deceive future generations. Moreover a people never stands alone; it exists among contemporary peoples whose history is blended with its own, and even were it capable of unanimous falsification, it would inevitably call forth the protestation of the very age under whose eyes it would have inaugurated its conspiracy.

The second condition of writing, in order for it to attain to the state of history, is that it must bear upon public events. Every fact that is not public does not belong to the domain of history, for the reason I have just given; for who has witnessed a fact that is not public? a single man, three men if you will, but history cannot be based upon the testimony either of a single man, or of three men; this is not history, it is only memory. Memory bears upon private facts, whilst history bears upon public events. For example, that Louis XIV. conquered Flanders, Alsace, Lorraine, that he joined these provinces to the kingdom of France, first by force of arms, then by treaties, is history; these are events which interested France and all the nations of Europe, and which had a hundred millions of men for spectators. But that Louis XIV. in his chamber at Versailles said something in presence of M. le Duc de Saint Simon, which is related in the works of that talented person, is nothing more than memory. Doubtless this secondary element enters largely into the formation of the annals of the human race, because we should not be satisfied with recitals wherein only the main features of historical architecture would be visible; we are attracted more even by the private details than by the general movements of the world: they approach nearer to our personal existence, and cause the most eminent personages of past times to descend even to us. Moreover, although destitute of the solemn certainty of history, they are not always without a grave sanction, although of an inferior order; private acts become interwoven with public acts; numerous concurring witnesses establishes each other's statements; and the whole advances in a manner not too unequal. Nevertheless, as soon as absolute historical certainty is aspired to, it is necessary to separate the two elements, and to give to the former, by that separation, all its force and all its lustre.

The third condition necessary to raise writing to the state of history, is that the events should blend together and form a public and general web. Nothing is isolated in the events of this world; they are connected with each other by a chain of succession similar to that which unites ideas in the logical tissue of a discourse. History should reproduce that continuous generation in such a manner that all the facts it relates should enter naturally into the course of things of which the progressive whole constitutes the life of the human race. A solitary fact is not a historical fact; it has no real place, it floats in air. Still much less should we give this name to a fact which cannot take its place in the general web of history without deranging its whole economy; this is the infallible sign of imposture. The force of history, like the force of every other real order is in its completeness and unity. When a man stands alone, he is nothing; when a fact stands alone, it is nothing. But let a man enter into association with others, they form a family, a people, the whole human race. And, in like manner, when a fact enters into historical association with others, and not with others only, but with all the rest, let it become necessary to the general web of history, so that history cannot be constructed without that fact, then it possesses not only the force of a historical fact, but the force of all history; we must accept it or deny the entire life of the human race.

The three elements of history are, then, public writing, public events, public web of events; and when these three elements are united, I affirm that history exists, and that it cannot be resisted without resisting the very force of common sense. In effect, gentlemen, for history to be false in this case see what must be possible: that a man, no matter who, relating in public events of a public nature, those events supposed to be false must be received as true, and, notwithstanding their falsity, be interwoven in the general web of history. Now this is altogether impossible, and nothing is more easy than to prove it to you. Allow me only one supposition. I suppose that to-morrow morning it may please me to publish a work the substance of which I thus sum up. On the 1st of January, 1847, France declared war against the three great continental powers of Europe. The object of this war was to re-establish the rights of nations and faith in treaties compromised by acts of violence. The hostile armies met on the plains of Mayence. France had six hundred thousand men under arms, the enemy had a million. The battle lasted ten consecutive days; on the morning of the tenth day the French were victorious. The plenipotentiaries of Europe assembled at Mayence, and signed a treaty which put an end to the war by a new partition of the European continent.

I ask you, gentlemen, do you believe that this political romance would have any chance of imposing upon posterity? Is it not manifest that France would treat it with the deepest scorn? If France accepted it, is it not manifest that the whole of Europe would hold it up to public derision? And if, by an act of universal folly, France and Europe consented to invest it with an absurd authority, is it not manifest that it would be found impossible to introduce it into the web of history, since the state of all contemporary affairs, and, consequently, of all future affairs, would be in contradiction with that pretended war and that fictitious treaty? To sustain falsehood, perpetual falsehood is necessary; and the conspiracy of a single moment against truth would require a conspiracy continued to the end of the world. The impossibility of such a concurrence and of such perseverance in a universal imposture is not only a moral impossibility, but a metaphysical and an absolute impossibility.

Now, gentlemen, to whatever epoch in the history of mankind we may turn, that impossibility would be the same. In all times and places, public writing describing public events which naturally range themselves in the general course of history would be authentic and true, because in all times and places it would have been impossible under such circumstances to deceive the human race in regard to its own life, or to persuade it to deceive itself without object and against all reason. And—mark it well, gentlemen—history once existing, time has not the privilege of lessening its force; so far from lessening, it confirms it. I say, first, that it does not lessen its force; and as proof I propose this to you: Think of Cæsar, then think of Louis XIV., and ask yourselves whether the historical certainty of Louis XIV. and the historical certainty of Cæsar differ in the slightest degree in your mind. Evidently, they do not differ; and yet seventeen centuries separate Louis XIV. from Cæsar. But those seventeen centuries vanish from your thought by the electrical glance which suddenly carries it from the one to the other, and causes it to perceive not only that the historical basis of Cæsar is the same as the historical basis of Louis XIV., but also that in doubting in regard to the first it would be needful to doubt the second, since without Cæsar history would lose all its connection, and therewith the principal cause of its reality. I say still more, I say that time confirms, instead of lessening the certainty of history. And why so? Because time at every step unfolds the historical canvas, and because each point of history entering into participation with the united force of the whole, the more that force increases by the repercussion of events upon each other, the more each particular point becomes settled, sustained and extended. Thus, Moses has been consolidated by Jesus Christ; for although Moses wrote publicly on public events, the web of history was short in his time, and wanted breadth; and when Jesus Christ took his place there, his presence lighted up the Mosaic past, as the Christian future had in its turn to reflect back again even to Jesus Christ. Whence it follows that we do not advance a step in the present time without again bearing to Moses the glory of a new confirmation, because in all that we do he supports us, and we in our turn explain all that he has done. The thread of history unceasingly goes and returns from the past to the future, from the future to the past; and that which we see with our eyes will be more clear to our posterity than it is to us, because upon the canvas which represents us they will complete designs which have not yet left the hands of the workmen. Like a building that covers its foundations, so is history; as land that grows firm by being trodden upon, so also is history under the footsteps of generations. In a word, time, which seemed the greatest enemy of history, as soon as history is founded, protects and consolidates it.

But does history exist? Is all that we have just said anything but a magnificent speculation? Does the human race know its own life? Is there in the world a history of the world? This, gentlemen, is to ask if there exist public writings containing a long web of public events; now these writings and this web of events are before your eyes. Mankind learns its primitive life by certain fundamental traditions collected in due time and confirmed by their universality; it learns its subsequent life from Moses by an unbroken history which advanced in constant development. From Moses to Herodotus is the dawn of history; from Herodotus to Tacitus its morning; Tacitus is its noon, and that noonday still lasts. It is even become more striking for the last three centuries, through a celebrated invention which has greatly increased the publicity and immortality of writing. As God had given writing to our fathers when tradition was in danger of growing obscure, he gave printing to them when writing itself was also menaced with becoming forgotten and confused from the superabundance of documents. Printing saved history fifteen hundred years after Jesus Christ, as writing saved tradition fifteen hundred years before him.

Such being the case, gentlemen, and history having existed for thirty centuries, it remains to be seen whether Jesus Christ does or does not form a part of history. I affirm that he is in history, and that none other in the world holds in it a place more important or more certain than his own.

What have I to do, gentlemen, in order to prove this? Evidently three things: I have to show that the life of Jesus Christ is contained in a public writing, that it is a tissue of public events, and that it enters naturally into the public web of history.

Now the life of Jesus Christ is contained in the Gospels, and the Gospels form a public writing; this is my first proposition. But you at once ask me where I find the proof that the Gospels form a public writing. Is it not, say you, in the Gospels themselves? And do you not thus prove the question by another question? Gentlemen, if the

Gospels commenced or formed the whole of history it would, perhaps, be difficult to reply to you; but you have not, I think, so soon forgotten that history existed before Jesus Christ; and God, who willed to give us the certainty of the existence and works of his Son, had apparently prepared the ground upon which we were one day to meet him. That ground is history; and at the time in which the life of Jesus Christ is placed, that is to say about the time of Augustus, history held a position in the world which did not depend upon us. It is not Catholics who make history; it is made without us and against us. It was in the hands of our enemies, and if we then began the history of the Church, that of the world continued its course upon a plan which was not ours, and in which no power was reserved to us. Now this is the history that I invoke to establish the publicity of the Gospels; and first of all I rest upon an observation which I consider fundamental; the Gospels, I say, were public writings, because they belonged to a public doctrinal society.

That the first Christians formed a doctrinal society is clear of itself; that that society was public is also beyond doubt; nevertheless it is necessary to establish this in the most positive manner, for it is the groundwork of the whole matter. It can indeed be conceived that a few men, secretly united, and preaching a secret doctrine, may have been able secretly to prepare a mysterious book, which had not been subject to any investigation, and which was spread from hand to hand, gaining authority with time. But if the Christian community was from the very first public; if, from the morrow of the death of Christ, his Apostles appeared in the public places of Judæa, and soon after in the public places of the Roman empire, provoking, not an occult war, but a visible and notorious struggle; if they said boldly to the Jews: "Jesus of Nazareth, a man approved of God among you, by miracles and wonders and signs, which God did by him in the midst of you, as you also know; this same being delivered up, by the determinate counsel and foreknowledge of God, you, by the hands of wicked men, have crucified and slain. Whom God hath raised up;"[1] if, being dragged before all the tribunals of the empire, when asked who they were, they answered: We are Christians, that is to say, the children of Christ, who has

---

[1] Acts ii. 22-24.

been put to death, but whom the arm of God—more powerful than all the conspiracies of men—has raised from his tomb, and elevated to be for ever the head and chief of all nations; if they said this, if it be certain that they said this—certain, not only from our writings, but from writings derived from strangers, from our enemies, by a multitude of documents—I shall have the right to conclude that the Christian society, at its beginning, was a public society, and that, differing from so many things formed in secret—because they have no faith in their strength and legitimacy—the Catholic Church began in publicity, as she has continued in publicity.

Let us come to the proof, and hear Tacitus, the most celebrated of historians—Tacitus, charged by God to grave in history the certificate of the birth and death of his only Son Jesus Christ. Twenty-seven years after that great drama of Calvary, Nero was pleased to burn Rome; and to hide the horror of that abominable action, he caused to be seized, says Tacitus, an "immense multitude of men"—INGENS MULTITUDO. Who were those men? Tacitus defines them: they were men "whom the common people called Christians"—QUOS VULGUS CHRISTIANOS APELLAbat. Remark this word vulgus; twenty-seven years after the death of Christ the name of his disciples was common in Rome, the capital of the world. But what were Christians? Tacitus tells us: "the author of this name was Christ"— auctor nominis hujus Christus. You hear, gentlemen, you hear; and the date of this text, which has never been contested by any one, is authentic; it is marked by the burning of Rome, in the year 64 of the Christian era, that is to say, twenty-seven years after the death of Jesus Christ. But is this all? No; you will hear more, you will hear the Apostles' Creed, written by the pen and with the ink of Tacitus. The historian had to say who Christ was; he continues, then: "They derived their name and origin from Christ, who, in the reign of Tiberius, had suffered death by the sentence of the procurator Pontius Pilate" —auctor nominis hujus Christus, qui, Tiberio imperitante, per procuratorem Pontium Pilatum supplicio affectus erat. Once more, is it Tacitus who speaks, or is it the Apostles' Creed? The Apostles' Creed says: Qui passus est sub Pontio Pilato; Tacitus says: Qui per procuratorem Pontium Pilatum supplicio affectus erat. It is indeed Tacitus—a stranger, a pagan, a man who, in writing these things in indestructible memorials, did not even know what he said. And what said he of the Christians, of that immense multitude whom the common people called Christians? He said this of them, in the same text: "For a while this dire superstition was checked; but it again burst forth, and not only spread itself over Judæa, the first seat of this evil, but even in Rome"—REPRESSAQUE IN PRÆSENS EXITIALIS SUPERSTITIO RURSUS ERUMPEBAT, NON MODO PER JUDÆAM ORIGINEM HUJUS MALI, SED PER URBEM ETIAM. What a text, gentlemen! what precision! what matter in two lines! Twenty-seven years, then, after the death of Christ, the Christians formed an immense multitude in Rome, they were commonly known by their true name; even before this epoch they had already been repressed by public authority, but that repression did not hinder them from spreading with such power, that Tacitus calls it an irruption; they appeared before the tribunals, and there bore testimony to their faith; for Tacitus adds that they were seized "upon their own avowal"—PRIMO CORREPTI QUI FATEBANTUR. They were "odious to all"—INVISOS: and their morals differed so much from general morals that, according to the remark of the historian, "they were less convicted of the crime of revolt than of hatred of the human kind"—HAUD PERINDE IN CRIMINE INCENDII, QUAM ODIO HUMANI GENERIS CONVICTI SUNT.² And Tacitus knew all this: he knew the life of Jesus Christ; he knew Pontius Pilate; the drama of Calvary was present to him.

Would you have another proof of the public life of Christians from the very origin of Christianity? God and history will not refuse it to you. In the year 98 of the Christian era—sixty-one years after the death of Jesus Christ—Trajan mounts the throne; and history brings us a letter of one of his proconsuls on the subject of the Christians, the proconsul of Bithynia and Pontus, Pliny the Younger, a celebrated man. For, observe, gentlemen, when God wills to write history, he is not unskilful in choosing his historians. We have just heard Tacitus; let us now hear Pliny the Younger, in an official letter to Trajan. He writes to the emperor to consult him about the measures to be taken against Christians; for, says he, "I have never had to deal with cases of this kind, and I know not what it is the custom to

---

² "Annals," book 15.

pursue and punish in them, or in what degree. I have no little difficulty in ascertaining whether it is needful to take account of difference of age or to be indifferent to it; whether pardon is to be granted on repentance, or whether it is useless to cease to be a Christian after having once professed Christianity; whether it is the name which is to be pursued, even when exempt from crime, or the crime attached to the name." What questions, gentlemen, for an able and good man! A name criminal! Crimes attached to a name! But what could he do? Pliny found in his way customs already inveterate against a society of men in open struggle with the Roman empire; and we perceive, even in the absurd things which he says, a desire to be as lenient as possible without offending the emperor. His letter ends with the remark, "that a great number of persons of every age, rank, and sex were compromised, and that others would be; that not only the cities, but the towns and villages, were overrun with that contagious superstition; that, in fine, the deserted temples, and the sacred ceremonies which had for a long time been interrupted, began to revive, in consequence of the measures taken against the Christians."

This picture, gentlemen, joined to that of Tacitus, leaves no doubt upon the capital point before us, namely, that from the origin of Christianity, the Christians lived in a publicly-constituted society. And, moreover, the very result obtained by them in the short space of three centuries is a superabundant proof of it. At the end of three centuries, the Christians were masters of the Roman empire; they bore to the throne the first Cæsar who embraced their faith, and, not content with this prodigy of their power, they said to Constantine: Withdraw to the Bosphorus, for here, in Rome, the chair of St. Peter, the fisherman of Gallilee, must be placed. And Constantine, from instinctive obedience to that unexpressed command of Providence, withdrew, and so bore, even to the borders of the Euxine, a proof, still subsisting, of the social mission of Jesus Christ. Now, gentlemen, no secret society has ever been capable of such success. All that begins in secret is accomplished in secret. When men speak to you of a secret society, it is as if they told you that nothing had formed an association. Doubtless these secret conspiracies may work secretly, shake the foundations of states, prepare the day of ruins; but they never attain to a regulated and public life. All that begins in darkness is struck with incapacity to live in open air and in open day. Therefore the attainment of empire by the Christian society, under Constantine, is of itself a sufficient proof that the Christian work was a constantly public work.

But if the first Christians formed a public society, and at the same time a doctrinal society, it necessarily follows that their writings were public. Endeavor to conceive a public doctrinal society which hides its writings; you will never succeed. For how would it be public, if it did not boldly proclaim what it believed, and how would it proclaim what it believed, if it secreted its writings, and those even which formed the foundation of its faith? Although the Gospels may not have been written on the very instant after the death and resurrection of Jesus Christ, they were published over the whole world by the preaching of the Apostles, and when they appeared successively, the young and living tradition became blended with them in one and the same authenticity. A contest of nearly three hundred years began upon the very text of the Gospels between Catholics on one hand, and heretics and philosophers on the other. This contest has left very numerous monuments. We see, then, Celsus and Porphyry following step by step upon the Gospels, the life of the Saviour. They do not dispute their publicity or their authenticity. Heretics do something more. Not only do they discuss upon the text consecrated by the adhesion of the Church, but they fabricate for themselves apocryphal Gospels to oppose them to the approved Gospels, so true is it that the whole discussion bore upon those fundamental texts. They were simple enough to make for themselves an arm against us of apocryphal Gospels, that is to say, to invoke against Jesus Christ books wherein the principal mysteries of his life and death were recognized, and where the very alteration of certain passages served but to prove so much the more the truth of the whole. It is very natural that great publicity should call forth counterfeits; this is even the greatest sign of success. Every idea, every style, every fashion that succeeds, raises up a cloud of imitators or speculators. But what is that to the man or to the thing which is the object of such effort? At least, it is not publicity which suffers from it; now, the publicity of the life of Jesus Christ by the Gospels and the primitive Christian books is precisely the point that I de sired to establish, and I do not think you will require more from me.

The life of Jesus Christ was, from the first, surrounded by immense publicity. His disciples, from the first, formed a public society; their profession of faith, their writings filled all the tribunals and all the schools of the earth; and finally, in three centuries, the emperor was publicly Christian, and the vicar of Jesus Christ was publicly seated in Rome. All this is as certain in profane history as in Christian history. This first point is gained.

As to the events which compose the very life of Jesus Christ, their nature is also that of manifest and striking publicity. What was in question? Was it a philosopher teaching certain disciples under a porch or in a garden? Was it but a Socrates, however celebrated he may be? No; it was a question of a man, the founder of a new religion, a thing that touched all—traditions, laws, customs, sentiments, even the most sacred interests; it was of a man the founder of an exclusive religion, and who designed nothing less than the overthrow of all existing religious and sacerdotal bodies; it was of a man working, it was said, in public unheard-of miracles, and accompanied everywhere by an innumerable multitude, attracted by his works and his doctrine; it was of a man called before the supreme tribunal of his country, condemned, put to death, and afterwards, it was said, raised again from the dead, and who sent his disciples to the moral conquest of the world; it was of a man having succeeded in raising up an unshaken faith in the hearts of a multitude of men of all nations, and become, by his name alone, the rallying-point of a new society. If ever there were public events, assuredly they were these.

And these events, which contradicted all the past life of the human race—which must, consequently, if they were false, have been rejected from the general web of history by an invincible impossibility of ever forming a part therein—have they or have they not taken their place in that rigorous chain of the human life during three thousand years? They have done more than this, gentlemen; without them history is an incomprehensible enigma. What, indeed, is the principal question of history, from Moses to Pius IX., those two extreme terms of the world's annals? Is it the rise and fall of the empires of Assyria, the Trojan war, the conquests of Alexander, the for tunes of the Romans, the rise of modern nations, the discovery of America, the progress of science and history in modern times? No; none of these questions, however vast they may be, is the principal question of history, the one that embraces the totality of the three thousand years that live in the memory of mankind. The principal question, because it contains all, the past, the present, and the future, is this: the world having lived in idolatry in the times before Augustus, how has it become Christian since his time? These are the two sides that divide all history, the side of antiquity, and the side of later ages; the one idolater, plunged into the most licentious materialism; the other Christian, purified at the sources of a complete spirituality. In the ancient world the flesh publicly prevailed over the spirit; in the present, the spirit publicly prevails over the flesh. What has caused this? Who has produced a change so great and so general in extent between the two periods of mankind? Who has so greatly modified the human form and the course of history? Your fathers adored idols; you, their posterity, descended from them by a corrupted blood, you adore Jesus Christ. Your fathers were materialists even in their worship; you are spiritualists even in your passions. Your fathers denied all that you believe; you deny all that they believed. Again I ask what is the reason of this? There are no events without causes in history, any more than there is movement without a motive power in mathematics. What is the historical cause which converted the idolatrous world into the Christian world, which gave Charlemagne as a successor to Nero? You are compelled to know or at least to seek it. We Catholics say that this prodigious change corresponds to the appearance upon earth of a man who called himself the Son of God, sent to take away the sins of the world—who preached humility, purity, penance, gentleness, peace; who lived piously among the poor and lowly; who died on a cross, with his arms extended over us to bless us; who left us his teaching and his example in the Gospel; and who, having thus touched the souls of many, subdued their pride and corrected their senses, has left in them a tranquil joy so marvellous that its perfume has spread to the ends of the world, and has won even sensuality. We say this. Yes, a man, a single man, has founded the empire of Christians upon the ruins of the idolatrous empire; and we do not marvel thereat, because we have remarked in history that all good as well as all evil invariably springs from a single principle, from a man, the depositary of the hidden force of the demon, or of the invisible force of God. We say this, and we base our declaration upon uninterrupted monuments which begin with Moses and reach to us; we appeal also to a publicity of thirty-two consecutive centuries; we join together the Jewish people, Jesus Christ, the Catholic Church, or rather we do not join these, they appear before us closely linked together in a course of things sustained the one by the other; we appeal, in fine, to the whole web of history, and in the name of that immense monument which it is absolutely necessary to admit and to explain, we say to you: Jesus Christ is the supreme expression of history, he is its key and its revelation. Not only does he form a part of history, he has taken his place in it in the midst of all its events, without difficulty and without effort, but history is not possible without him. Endeavor, in following the line of these monuments, to pass from the ancient to the new world, and to explain to yourselves how, without Jesus Christ, the Pope has replaced the Cæsars at the Vatican. Is it possible to do this? And if a gleam of good faith remain in the depths of your soul, will you not be compelled to say with us: Yes, it is in Christ on Calvary, in that blood which was shed, that the renovation of the human race began.

Therefore, gentlemen, before our epoch, none dared to deny the historical reality of Jesus Christ, not one. Before you, long before you, Jesus Christ had enemies, for before you pride existed, and pride is the chief enemy of Jesus Christ. Before you, Jesus Christ had enemies, for before you sensuality existed, and sensuality is the second enemy of Jesus Christ. Before you, Jesus Christ had enemies, for before you egotism existed, and egotism is the third enemy of Jesus Christ. And yet, when he appeared for the first time, when he came with his cross to sap your pride, to insult your senses, to drag down your egotism to the very dust, what was said to him? Pride, sensuality, egotism, had then, as now, able men in their service—Celsus, Porphyry, all the Alexandrian school, and the lovers of this life, and the throng of courtiers, ever ready to find in truth a secret enemy to power. What said they of Christ? They pursued him by putting his followers to death; by deriding his life; by disputing his dogmas; by oppression called to the help of a cause which betrayed liberty; but their books, subsisting in a thousand remains by the aid of printing—which I just now called the salvation of history—their books confirm him; not one of them has denied the reality of the life of Jesus Christ. You alone, coming eighteen centuries after, and thinking that time, which confirms history, is its destroyer, you have dared to battle against the very light of the sun, hoping that every negation is at least a shadow, and that human folly, seeking a refuge against the severity of Jesus Christ, would accept of any arm as a defence, and of any shield as a protection. You have deceived yourselves. History subsists in spite of negation, as the heart of man subsists in spite of the debauchery of the senses; and Jesus Christ remains under the shelter of unexampled publicity, and of a necessity to which there is no counterpoise, upon the summit of history.

Nevertheless, as a last hope you say to me: If it were a question of human events only, such as those of which the ordinary annals of nations are composed, it is manifest that the life of Jesus Christ contained in the Gospels would be beyond all discussion. But in that life it is a question of events which bear no comparison with those we habitually witness. It is a question of a God who made himself man, who died and rose again; how is it possible for us to admit such strange things upon a mass of human evidence? For, in fine, public writings, public events, the public and general web of history, all this assemblage of proofs is purely human; and it is upon this mortal foundation that you base a history where all is superhuman. The base must evidently sink under such a weight.

Gentlemen, I do not undervalue the force of that objection. Yes; I understand that when it is a question of the history of a God it needs another pen than that which traces the history of the greatest man in the world; this is true. But I also believe that God has solved this objection by creating for his only Son, Jesus Christ, a history which is not human, that is to say, which, in its proportions, is so much above the nothingness of man, that the ordinary power of history would evidently not have sufficed for it. Where indeed will you find such connection as that of the Jewish people, Jesus Christ, and the Catholic Church? Where is there anything to be compared with it? And, moreover—without returning to what has already been said—where amongst all the histories known to you, do you find any which for three centuries had witnesses who gave to it the testimony of their blood? Where are the witnesses who have given their lives in favor of the authenticity of the greatest men or the greatest events? Who died to certify the history of Alexander? Who died to certify the history of Cæsar? Who? No one. No one in the world has ever shed his blood to add another degree of evidence to the historical certainty of anything whatever. Men leave history to take its course. But to form it with their blood, to cement historical testimony with human blood for three centuries, is what has never been witnessed, save on the part of Christians for Jesus Christ. We were interrogated during three centuries, and asked to declare who we were; we answered: Christians. They then said to us: Blaspheme the name of Christ; and we replied: We are Christians. They put us to death for this in frightful tortures; and in the hands of our executioners our last sigh exhaled, as a balm for the dying and a testimony for the living to all eternity, the name of Jesus Christ. We did not die for opinions, but for realities—the very name of martyrs proves it; and Pascal has well said: "I believe in witnesses who give the testimony of their blood." And although there may be presumption in attempting to speak better than Pascal, I shall however say something better: I believe in the human race dying for its faith.

Shall I give you another sign which shows the elevation of Jesus Christ, in history, above all history? Tell me which amongst the ancient peoples of the world, the most celebrated in your eyes, has left guardians upon his tomb to protect its history? Where are the survivors of the Assyrians, the Medes, the Greeks, the Romans? Where are they? What defunct people renders testimony to its life? One alone, the Jewish people, at the same time dead and living, a relic of the ancient world in the new, and a self-accusing witness in favor of Christ—by the Jews crucified. God has preserved them for us as an irreproachable witness; I produce them, they are there. Behold them! The blood is in their hands. And we also, Catholics, we, the Church, we are by their side, we speak with them and as loudly as they. As a living and a universal society we bear, in the wounds of our martyrs, the blood shed by us to render testimony to the history of Jesus Christ; and on their side, as a society, living also, universal also, the Jewish people bear blood which is not their own, but which is not less eloquent than ours. There are two witnesses here, and two streams of blood. Behold them! Look on the right hand and on the left of Christ, behold the people who crucified him, behold the people who sprang from his cross. They both speak the same thing to you, both, during eighteen centuries, suffer a martyrdom which is not the same, but which has the same source, both are enemies—they meet but in one single thing, Jesus Christ! Ah! you would defy God! Learn that when man defies God, his Providence inevitably prepares an answer for him, and you have just heard, on the subject of Jesus Christ, the answer he has given to you.

I conclude, gentlemen: to deny the historical reality of the life of Jesus Christ is an act of folly, an act of desperation. And you wonder perhaps why this has been done, directly or indirectly, with or without precaution. It is, because the historical reality of Jesus Christ once admitted, or taken for granted, the sentiment of his divinity begins to shine in the mind, and it is difficult not to yield more or less. It was necessary to gather clouds around an existence so remarkable, connected, moreover, with so many things which are remarkable also. Were the result of negation only to call forth proof of the fact, it would already have provoked discussion, and discussion is of value on unattackable ground; its prestige seems to be thereby lessened. It is better, in fine, to attempt something than to remain inactive. Then, hatred blinds, it renders the vision insensible to the clearest evidence; and, in this sense, it was fitting that the historical reality of Jesus Christ should be attacked, as a proof of the intellectual diminution of those who become his enemies. Truth gains by the attacks of the mind as by those of the body; and, tranquil in the inaccessible eyrie where God has placed her, sure of herself, however she may be attacked, she can say to man, imitating a celebrated line:

"*Contest,* if thou canst; and if thou dar'st, *consent!*"

THE EFFORTS OF RATIONALISM TO PERVERT THE LIFE OF JESUS CHRIST.

My Lord—Gentlemen,

In our last conference I proved to you the historical reality of Jesus Christ. But what is it to have proved to you the historical reality of Jesus Christ? Does it mean that a man called Jesus Christ undoubtedly lived at a certain epoch? If we have proved but this we shall have proved nothing, for a name is nothing. To prove the historical reality of a personage is to prove the reality of the living type which constitutes that personage. Thus, when I name Cæsar, I do not name an indifferent person, I name the Roman who, before Augustus, conquered and governed the Gauls, who, recalled by the Senate, passed the Rubicon, assumed the dictatorship, and at last fell under the daggers of a band of conspirators. So, also, when I name Jesus Christ, I name him who, in the time of Tiberius, preached a religious doctrine in Judæa, supported his preaching by acts, about which you reserve your judgment, but which were at least extraordinary, who was surrounded by disciples, and, after a condemnation followed by his death, was presented to the whole world as living, and who, in fine, founded that hierarchy, that dogma, that worship, that Catholic Church, which we see still living before our eyes. And to have proved the historical reality of Jesus Christ is to have proved the reality of this type whose leading features I have just traced.

I have done more, gentlemen; I have at the same time proved the authenticity of the Gospels. For a book is authentic when it is historical; and I have shown that the Gospels possess all the characters of history, that is to say, that they were public writings, containing public events adapted to the general and public web of the annals of the human race. This is its great authenticity. There is another, secondary and of little importance, which consists in knowing the precise date of a book and the exact name of its author. I place it below the former, because a book may have a certain date and a certain author without possessing any historical value, whilst a historical book bears with itself the date and the course of things authentically promulgated by invincible publicity. The Gospels are authentic in both ways, but as the first and great authenticity is of itself sufficient, I have confined myself chiefly to establishing it.

Perhaps in listening to me, gentlemen, you have asked yourselves whom I was addressing, why I took so much pains about a thing which did not seem to be contested. In this you would have deceived yourselves. Not only in a celebrated work on the " Origin of all Religions " has Dupuis denied the historical reality of Jesus Christ, but so also in some degree does every unbeliever, endeavoring to raise up clouds between his mind and that formidable figure of the Son of God manifest in the flesh. Hence it is that you hear it so blandly and so falsely repeated that no contemporary testimony, out of the Christian school, attests the presence of Jesus Christ upon the stage of history. Hence it is that the famous text of Flavius Josephus on the life and death of Christ has been made the object of so much suspicion. There are no unbelievers whom the historical certainty of the early times of Christianity does not disturb and importune, and who do not set a high value upon the slightest doubt in regard to it.

It was necessary then to take away this consolation from them—the more so, gentlemen, as in demonstrating to you the divinity of Jesus Christ I had previously supposed the authenticity of his person and history, and because if I had not retraced my steps in order definitely to establish this, the whole edifice of my demonstration would have rested upon a gratuitous hypothesis. Let us to-day complete the substitution of the reality for the hypothesis by treating of another effort of rationalism, no longer to destroy the life of Jesus Christ, but to pervert it. For, after having said or suggested that the life of Christ was a fable, rationalism itself perceived that it was too much to ask of human credulity; it feared the all-powerful light of common sense; and at the beginning of this century, not in England, not in France, but in Germany, a new system has been developed. The life of Christ, they say, is not a fable, but a myth. What is a myth? Is the life of Christ a myth? Such is, gentlemen, the object of this conference and of your attention.

Let us first clearly understand the causes which have kept rationalism from sanctioning, by its adhesion, the historical reality of Jesus Christ. Assuredly there remain many questions to solve, even when it is admitted that Jesus Christ lived, that his history is authentic, that publicity sheds the clearest light upon the origins of Christianity and Christendom. Yet, gentlemen, when we have advanced thus far, we immediately find ourselves before a very simple dilemma: either Jesus Christ and his apostles were sincere, or they were impostors; to say they were sincere is in the main to admit the divinity of their work; for, the reality of the life of Christ being established on the one hand, and the sincerity of their work being admitted on the other, we cannot, before the nature and the course of events which form its tissue, avoid this conclusion: Jesus Christ is God. If, on the contrary, it is affirmed that Jesus Christ and his apostles were impostors, the position is one which the mind will hardly accept. And why? Because all that belongs to Jesus Christ, all the apostles, all the martyrs, manifest the sincerity of man in its highest degree; because God has placed in the person of Jesus Christ, in the life of his apostles, in the death of his martyrs, a character of truthfulness which leaves no room for the supposition that all that beautiful history, for three whole centuries, is nothing but a mass of imposture steeped in blood. Moreover, Christianity is now sincere; it is impossible to accuse of falsehood the multitude of civilized men who believe in Jesus Christ, who profess to have the daily demonstration of his divinity, who say that, even independently of the Gospel history, the action alone of Christ upon them manifests its all-powerful reality; and it is the thesis of a celebrated German, who, having made the historical void around him, and inwardly verifying to his mind the influence of the Saviour of men, said to Germany: But I who live, who feel, who think, I live with Jesus Christ, I feel with Jesus Christ, I think with Jesus Christ; he raises me above myself, he purifies me, he gives me that which nothing in this world has ever given me; he is then more than myself, more than the world, more than the soul, he is God. Yes, we are sincere, and if all Christians do not prove their sincerity by their virtues, many of them at least render to Jesus Christ this testimony of their faith. Will you dare to charge them with hypocrisy? Will you dare to insult the hearts and actions of so great a number of men bound to you by so many ties? Hypocrites! And why? With what object? What pleasure is there in being chaste from hypocrisy? What a strange design, and what a strange salary for such a sacrifice! We are then sincere, and we are able to say of Jesus Christ, the spouse of our souls, that which *Pauline* said of *Polyeuctes*, and with the same feeling:

> "My spouse in dying has left me his light,
> I see, I know, I believe!"

But if Christianity is now sincere, how is it possible that, from the highest of all imposture, namely, that of assuming the name of God, this torrent, this sea of sincerity, should have spread its bays and horizons even to us, to the very centre of existing mankind? An impure cause cannot produce a pure effect, and if Christianity is now sincere, it was so yesterday, the day before, in the days of its youth, it was so in Jesus Christ, in the first heart whence it issued to fire our own and render it true. Or, if you deny the consequence under that form, recognize at least in Jesus Christ, in his apostles and martyrs, signs of sincerity still greater even than those of Christianity in the present time, and learn why unbelief needs to reject from history the primitive times of Christianity—fearing lest, having once given admission to them, they would too readily attain the crown of incontestable divinity. Yes, our ancestors, the unbelievers of France, showed the necessary boldness; they placed the question in its true light, and whosoever does not follow them, at all risk and peril, is a coward or an infant in the order of negation. Our fathers, here as elsewhere, advanced straight to the heart of things; with the native intrepidity of their minds, they comprehended that it was needful to deny all or to admit all. I laud them for it, for, after all, when men love error it is better to steer in it like Columbus than like those timid barks which fear to brave the ocean, and break up on the very edge of the shore. By advancing boldly, the end is sooner reached, and the very mind which pursued error has thus greater chances of entering in full sail into the harbor of truth.

German genius is not, it seems, endowed with this advantage of brightness and rapidity. It is this genius which has created the theory of the myth, around which it has hovered for fifty years. But what is a myth? Sweep away the vaulted roof of this cathedral, and gaze upon that other vault of which Pascal said: "The eternal silence of that unknown space terrifies me." Beyond the luminaries which your eye easily discovers there as it were on the extreme frontier of space, you will still perceive an array of unknown stars. Are they the result of vision deceived by distance? Have they a total subsistence? Or rather is the cause of their apparition at the same time an optical illusion and a certain reality? So will it be if, instead of exploring the profound regions of the firmament, you cast a prying glance upon the frontiers of antiquity. You will find there recitals which will trouble your mind, uncertain whether to reject or to admit them. I take Prometheus, for example. You all know the story of Prometheus—that daring man who stole fire from heaven, and whom Jupiter, in punishment for so great a sacrilege, caused to be chained to a rock, where his liver is devoured by a vulture. Antiquity was full of this story, upon which Æschylus formed one of the most remarkable tragedies of the Greek stage. What in fact was Prometheus? Was it a pure fable? It is very difficult to think so, gentlemen; man always founds the objects of his belief upon some reality, and when these objects have a universal character it is not logical to treat them with absolute disdain. But, on another hand, would you range the story of Prometheus in history? This is equally impossible. How can we admit that a man stole fire from heaven, that God chained him to a rock, and that his liver, never diminishing, was ever preyed upon there by an insatiable vulture? We are here evidently between fable and history. An event relative to the religious destinies of the human race occurred in the depths of primordial ages; the people carried its remembrances in their emigrations; but as the shadow of the past deepened upon the world the true physiognomy of that antique tragedy lost its clearness; imagination came to the help of memory, and Prometheus chained to his rock became the popular expression of a great crime followed by a great expiation. This is a myth. A myth is a fact transfigured by an idea; and the frontiers of antiquity—I repeat the expression—appear to us as it were guarded by a legion of myths, which are all adulterated expressions of certain truths.

Such being the case, says Dr. Strauss—one of the most celebrated members of the mythic school—why should not Jesus Christ be a myth? Why should not the Gospels be a collection of myths, that is to say, of real facts transfigured by ideas? Let us see if this be not possible; and, in the second place, if it be not real.

That it is possible, in the first place, analogy leaves us hardly room for doubt. Is there a religion, whether idolatry, or Brahminism or Buddhism, which subsists otherwise than by a vast assemblage of facts and ideas adulterated the one by the other? If you deny this, Christians, you will inflict a heavy blow upon yourselves. For you would thereby affirm that mankind is so wanting in common sense as to be capable of adoring for centuries fables devoid of every kind of foundation, traditional or ideal. Evidently you cannot deny it; you must admit, under pain of wounding your own selves, that wherever men have bent the knee with some universality and perpetuity they have had before them facts incrusted in conceptions. But if this be the general phenomenon, why may not Christianity have been produced under the empire of the same law? Doubtless Christians adore realities; Jesus Christ is a reality; but with the course of time and the fascination of a preconceived idea, as in all occasions of like nature, the primordial fact, although certain, has undergone modifications in the idea of its adorers which take it from pure history and range it in the category of myths. That Jesus Christ has not undergone so complete a transformation as the more distant events of remote antiquity, may be readily granted; but the degree of more or less is a secondary question only; and it nevertheless remains that the person of Christ and the Christian event are comprised in the general law which links to the myth all known religions.

So much the less is this to be doubted, as the publication of the Gospels is not contemporary with Jesus Christ. From the very avowal of Christians, many years of tradition and preaching preceded the era of the evangelical writings; and, if we come to exact criticism, we shall not be able to place the assured reign of the New Testament before the middle of the second century. What a space left to the imagination and to faith for transforming Jesus Christ!

It is especially worthy of remark that this transformation was so much the more easy, as the Messianic idea pre-existed Jesus Christ. Long before he appeared, that idea flowed in the veins of the Jewish people; a vast number of men, attentive to the voice of the prophets, looked for the Messiah who was to come; and after Christ had attributed this mission to himself, it was natural that all its features should be applied to him. The Messianic idea was the mould in which, for three centuries, the myth of Jesus Christ was formed. Jesus Christ had, so to say, but to leave things to their own course, and when he died his life entered of itself, like matter in fusion, into the mould of the Messianic idea, whence at length it came forth such as it now is before the astonished eyes of generations.

Analogy, the time, the preconceived idea of the Messiah, all these circumstances lead to the conclusion that Christianity may have been formed, like all the religions of antiquity, by the principle of mythical transfiguration. But a closer examination will lead us far beyond that conclusion, and cause us to perceive in the New Testament all the characters of an accomplished myth.

In the first place, the life of Jesus Christ, as related in the Gospels, is stamped with a character of continuous marvel. From the angel who announced his conception in the womb of the Virgin Mary, up to his resurrection and ascension, not a single event in the whole of that existence is conformable with the course of nature. Every word developes a prodigy, every step is a miracle, and the miracle seems constantly struggling to surpass itself and to confound the last hopes of reason. Now, the marvellous is precisely the inseparable companion of the myth, and its seat is the same. Where, in fact, do we find the marvellous? Is it before our eyes—near to us, in the modern world? Never. All that we see is simple and natural: general laws, whence proceeds a constant order, governing the world which is before us; God does not act in it by any sudden and capricious intervention, but he leaves to secondary causes their indissoluble succession. Where then do we find the marvellous? There even where we find the myth—in antiquity. Antiquity is the seat of the one and the other; and the myth itself is revealed to us only by the presence of the marvellous. For if nothing were marvellous in antiquity, all would be history. But what then is it that distinguishes the marvellous in regard to Jesus Christ from the marvellous elsewhere? In himself, nothing; as to place, nothing still, since that place is antiquity. Why, then, may we ask, do you divide antiquity in twain, and call one false and the other true? Why reject in the myth that which was marvellous before Jesus Christ, and raise to the rank of history the marvellous which is contemporary with him? Reason seizes no motive for this distinction, if it be not that you call the time of Jesus Christ a historical period, in opposition to other epochs which you call fabulous. But the marvellous is the very character that distinguishes fabulous from historical ages; for, without this, where would be the principle of their distinction?

In the second place, it is manifest, on the first reading of the Gospels, that they present no chronological suite, nothing which announces history, but that they are simple materials collected in minds at hazard, without the slightest attempt having been made to give them any appearance of harmony. All is in confusion and contradiction there. Dr. Strauss has had but to read and let his pen run freely, to form four volumes of the inconceivable blunders of which they are full. And we must not blame the evangelists for this; it is the very proof of their sincerity. They took the myth as they found it, vague, indefinite, contradictory—like all that comes from the gloomy confluence of facts and ideas. More than a century had passed over the life of Jesus Christ; shreds of that life had been carried from the east to the west, under the impression of sentiments and ideas of diverse origins; and, although the type possessed some unity because of the Messianic form which was the primitive starting-point, it was nevertheless impossible for the final elaboration of so many elements not to bear visible marks of disagreement and variety.

Such, gentlemen, is the reasoning of the mythic school. I believe I have not hidden any of its force from you; I do not like to depreciate the enemies of truth. Why should I? Were I to succeed for a moment in abusing your penetration and memory, on returning to your homes a glance at the work of Dr. Strauss would reveal to you my want of sincerity, and the cause I defend, for the half-hour it may have gained, would have lost a century in your minds. No, gentlemen, it is less than a duty, it is a pleasure to be sincere when we have truth on our side; and if the arguments of the mythic school have wanted force in passing by my mouth, it is because, after three months devoted to the study of them, it is not possible for me to impart to them more attractiveness and more authority. Do not, however, deceive yourselves; the work is as skilful as it could be. You perceive that the historical reality of Jesus Christ is no longer denied; they no longer rush to their destruction against the very constitution of history; and yet Jesus Christ, although remaining as a reality, is disarmed of the power of that position. On another hand, it is no longer necessary to combat the impression of sincerity which results from his life and that of his disciples. That sincerity is admitted. Jesus Christ believed in himself, and men believed in him. They believed in him before Cæsar, they believe in him before incredulity. Your fathers gave their blood for realities and ideas; you do the same. Only you do not properly understand them; and it is permitted, it is honorable, it is glorious, to live and die for things which we do not properly understand.

Gentlemen, I believe this exposition is sufficient. I will now meet this great engine of Germanic warfare.

Shall I deny the existence of myths? No, gentlemen; the myth appears to me historically as of all things in the world the most veritable. I admit that man, left to tradition during a long course of ages, ends by no longer clearly perceiving the limit and the primitive text of events. Like a picture before which the spectator constantly retreats, the human race retreats before the past; and however attentively it may be watched, at length it becomes obscure. The imagination, however, dwelling upon this now distant scene, adds new features to it, the idea governs the fact, and something is produced which is neither history nor fable, but that which we call a myth. Mythology is the assemblage of all the creations of the human mind between the gloom and the light of antiquity. For, remark where is the theatre of myths. It is antiquity, or rather it is tradition abandoned alone to the course of mankind, which bears it along in advancing and pressing onward. The seat of the myth is in pure tradition. But wherever writing appears, wherever there is a fixed recital, wherever the indelible record is placed before the eyes of generations, at that moment the mythic power of man vanishes. For then the reality remains before him in its true proportions, it remains in command of his imagination, and a thousand years can do no more against it than a single day. Never, since the time of Herodotus and Tacitus, has any one shown you myths in history. Has Charlemagne become a myth after a thousand years? Clovis after thirteen hundred years? Augustus, Cæsar, in retreating into the past, have they assumed any mythical appearance? No; the most distant point where the modern historian seeks to discover the myth is, for example, the beginning of Rome, Romulus and Remus. And why? Because although they approached writing, although it existed before them in other countries, it had not yet received the guardianship of Roman history. But, as soon as writing exists, as soon as it seizes the general web of history, the mythical mould is from that moment broken.

Now, Jesus Christ does not belong to the reign of tradition, but to the reign of writing. He was born at a period when writing was fully established, in a land where it was impossible for the myth to take root and grow. Providence had foreseen all and prepared all beforehand; and if you have sometimes wondered why Jesus Christ came so late, you now see a reason for it. He came so late not to be in antiquity, to have his place in the centre of writing; for he does not stand first there; he was careful to provide against being so placed; fifteen hundred years preceded him, and if you count only from Herodotus, five hundred years preceded him. Therefore he is modern, and even should the world last for numberless ages, as by means of writing all is present, since at a glance and with the rapidity of lightning we survey the whole chain of history,

Jesus Christ is ever new, standing in the full reality of the events which compose the known and certain life of the human race.

I might stop here, gentlemen; for you see clearly that the mythic engine is overthrown, since the fundamental condition of the myth, which is the absence of writing, is wanting in regard to Jesus Christ. Dr. Strauss himself expressly admits that the myth is not possible with writing, therefore he endeavors to strip Jesus Christ of the scriptural character by placing at as remote a period as possible the publication of the Gospels. We shall soon see the weakness of that resource, if you will permit me to follow step by step the trace of his reasoning.

Analogy, says he, is against Jesus Christ, since the myth is the basis of all known religions. This I deny. The myth is the basis of all the religions of antiquity, save the Mosaic, because all those religions plunged their roots in a tradition of which writing had not fixed the shadows, and so rendered deflections impossible. But writing having appeared, even the false religions, such as that of Mahomet, have taken a historical consistency which manifestly separates them from the priesthoods and corrupted dogmas of antiquity. The difference is clear. This is why we Christians, and you who fight against Christianity, never think of combating Mahomet by making a myth of his person, and of the Koran a mythical compilation. The force of writing, under the empire of which he lived, interdicts to us even the thought of such chimerical temerity. We are constrained to avow that he is a real personage, that he wrote or dictated the Koran, organized Islamism; and our sole resource against his pretensions in regard to us is to treat him as an impostor, to say boldly to him: Thou hast lied! But here the difficulty is greater, the success much more costly; and this is why rationalism disputes with so much art the powerful reality of Christ. However this may be, the analogy which is invoked to spread over him the clouds of the myth is an analogy without foundation. A great line of demarcation separates into two hemispheres all known religions — the mythic hemisphere and the real hemisphere; the former contains all the religions formed in primitive times under the empire of floating traditions, the latter contains the true or false religions which writing has enchained in a settled history and dogma. To reject the former, it suffices to oppose to them their mythical nature; to reject the latter, it is necessary to enter into the discussion of their historical, intellectual, moral, and social value.

It is true that the scriptural character of Jesus Christ is contested, but how? Because, say they, it is impossible to prove that the promulgation of the Gospels took place before the year 150 of the Christian era, whence it follows that the type of Christ floated, during more than a century, at the mercy of tradition. Suppose, gentlemen, that I admit this; suppose that I admit that our Gospels did not appear before the year 150. Bear in mind that before 150 writing existed elsewhere than in the Christian school; it existed among the Jews, the Greeks, the Romans; over the whole space upon which the question of Christianity was disputed; history was founded by the publicity and immutability of the monuments. Before 150, Jesus Christ, dead and risen again, was announced in all the synagogues that covered the surface of the Roman world, and even beyond it; he was publicly announced in the palace of the Cæsars, and in the pretorium of all the proconsuls. Before 150, I have cited Tacitus and Pliny the Younger, who attest that it was so.

That preaching, those testimonies, those discussions, that struggle, that blood, all was public, was written; it was not a dead tradition left to the chances of time and imagination during a thousand years of indifference and peace. At the same moment men gave their teaching and their life; and three communities together, supremely interested in what was passing—the Christian community, the Jewish, and the Roman — met upon the battle-field, the traditional limit of which you circumscribe within the period of little more than a century. What! those Jews to whom it was said: You have killed Jesus Christ; those princes and those presidents whose orders were trampled under foot in the name of Jesus Christ; not one of them perceived that it was all only a myth in the state of formation? No; all was steeped in blood, and consequently in reality; all was in discussion, and consequently in the strength and glory of publicity, which is the foundation of all history. It matters little then what date the Gospels bear, for history supports the Gospels. If they did not appear before a hundred and twenty years after Jesus Christ, they existed before they appeared, they lived in the mouth of the apostles, in the blood of the martyrs, in the hatred of the world, in the breasts of millions of men who confessed Jesus Christ dead and risen again! What a pitiable resource, gentlemen, what weakness! To compare a religion whose origin is so public and militant, and whose tradition could have preceded writing only a hundred and twenty years, to those religions without history, plunged for two thousand years in the still waters of a tradition which was confided to no one, and for which no one ever gave a drop of his blood!

I hardly need to tell you, gentlemen, that we do not accept the date which they attempt to assign to the promulgation of the Gospels. The Gospels are public writings, containing public facts which enter into the public web of history; they bear the names of three apostles, and of a celebrated disciple, who were public men in a public society; now, it is impossible that such an attribution, under such circumstances, should be contrary to truth. The mathematical laws of publicity do not permit it. The Gospels are apostles; they possess the value of their testimony, and the date of their life, that is to say, the date of a contemporary life, and the value of a contemporary testimony. This detail of authenticity blends itself with the general authenticity of the Christian origin, and is not separable therefrom. Judge yet once more of the relation existing between such monuments and the obscure myths emerging from the silent and dark abyss of remote antiquity.

In vain, in order to place Jesus Christ in a more remote period than his time, have they had recourse to the Messianic idea which prepared his coming. In the first place, the Messianic was not a myth; it appertained to a scriptural people, a people who wrote and who were written about; and the Messianic idea itself was a part of their writing. The idea and the fact were fixed. But even had Messianism primitively been a myth, it could no longer preserve that character in its application to Jesus Christ. For that application to Jesus Christ was modern; it took place at a scriptural and public epoch, and, consequently, whatever it may have been in the past, the myth disappeared in the broad day of Jesus Christ and his age. The real question extinguished the chimerical question.

There remain, gentlemen, the mythic characters which they pretend to discover in the very history of Jesus Christ. The first of these characters is the marvellous. The marvellous, say they, is the mythic character, properly so called; wherever it shows itself history disappears; for a miracle being impossible in itself, every narration containing it would evidently not be historical. Therefore, says Dr. Strauss, I overthrow your dogmatism by this single expression: The Gospel is a tissue of miracles, now miracles are impossible, their history is then impossible also, and consequently that history does not exist. It can be but a myth.

Whether a miracle be impossible or not, is a metaphysical question of which I have already treated, and to which I shall not return. But, at least, it is a question. You rationalists do not admit the possibility of the sovereign action of God in this world; we Christians admit that possibility. Now, we are men like yourselves, intelligent beings like yourselves; if you are numerous, we are more so than you; if you are learned, we are as learned as you. And whilst you deny the possibility of a miracle, we daily ask God to perform miracles, being fully persuaded that he thus manifests his power and goodness towards us, even in the present day. We go further, we do not comprehend the idea of God without the idea of a sovereignty able to manifest itself by the omnipotence of its action; so that, for us, the negation of the possibility of the miracle is the negation of the very idea of God. God, according to us, is miraculous in his nature; and if history ceases by miracles, we think that God ceases without them. You see that an abyss separates these two sentiments. What follows? It follows that the possibility of miracles is a question; and consequently to determine the reality of history by the presence or absence of miracles, is but to decide one question by another question—a mode of proceeding which is contrary to the rules of logic and common sense. What! documents are authentic, they are linked together and form a visible and continuous order, they blend with the whole course of the public life of mankind, they are irrefragable, certain, sacred, it is an act of folly to assail them; but the finger of God is seen in them, that power which created the world —and that is enough, history has disappeared! You will not ask me, gentlemen, even supposing that miracles may be problematical in themselves, to deny the certain because of the uncertain. We Christians admit the uncertain on the faith of the certain: each has his own logic.

Nevertheless, say they, the marvellous is the only character that distinguishes fable from history. It is not so, gentlemen; the line of demarcation between history and fable lies elsewhere; it lies in the difference between things without continuity and without any public monuments, and things which possess continuity, and are firmly based on all sides upon publicity. I have already said this; I shall not repeat it.

Is Dr. Strauss more fortunate in that which forms the basis of his work—the exposure of innumerable mistakes and contradictions of our evangelists? I think not. I have read his work with attention and labor, and I did so in this manner. After having studied a paragraph—always a very long one—and there are a hundred and forty-nine of them, filling four volumes, I closed the book in order to recover a little from fatigue and from a kind of involuntary terror caused by the abundance of erudition. Then, opening the Gospel—which I kissed respectfully —I read the texts under discussion, to see if by the simple aid of ordinary literature, and without the help of any commentators, I could not succeed in unravelling the difficulty. With the exception of three or four passages, I have never required more than ten minutes to dissipate the charm of vain knowledge, and to smile within myself at the powerlessness to which God has condemned error. I cannot, gentlemen, pass in review before you all that legion of texts distorted by rationalism; I will limit myself to two examples taken at hazard.

Saint Luke, having to narrate the birth of Jesus Christ at Bethlehem, away from the country of his parents, writes in these terms: "And it came to pass that in those days there went out a decree from Cæsar Augustus, that the whole world should be enrolled; this enrolling was first made by Cyrinus the governor of Syria." Upon this Dr. Strauss, after having first shown very learnedly that the enrolling was not possible, opens the "Judaical Antiquities" of Flavius Josephus, and shows by a formal text that Cyrinus did not govern Syria until ten years after the birth of Jesus Christ. Judge what a triumph this was! Now, how was this difficulty to be solved? You think, perhaps, that we shall have to change a word or a letter? No; it is less than that. You all know the value of an accent in the Greek language; change then an accent, and see what will be the meaning of the evangelist: "And it came to pass that in those days there went out a decree from Cæsar Augustus that the whole world should be enrolled; this is the same first enrolling which was made by Cyrinus the governor of Syria." That is to say, that the order having been given to number the Roman empire, and the execution of that order having been commenced, it was not however accomplished until ten years after, under Cyrinus the governor of Syria. And if the sacred historian makes mention of the name of Cyrinus, it is precisely to give an authentic character to his declaration; for had he been content with saying: "There went out a decree from Cæsar Augustus that the whole world should be enrolled," it might have been said that the enrolling did not take place at the time of the birth of Christ. He anticipated the objection then by saying: "this is the same first enrolling which was made by Cyrinus the governor of Syria."

Here is another example: It is said, in regard to the resurrection of our Lord, that the holy women went to the tomb, according to St. Mark, the sun being then risen, and according to St. John, when it was yet dark. Dr. Strauss notices this contradiction amongst a great number which he pretends to discover in the event of the resurrection—and he does not fail to turn them to account. But how shall we solve this terrible difficulty? It suffices to comprehend that when a distance is to be reached early in the morning it is possible to start before sunrise, and to arrive at daybreak.

I assure you, gentlemen, that, save a very few passages, nothing has caused me any greater trouble. So that after the work had often left my hands from weariness, my hands fell from me again when I thought that this was learning, German learning—that learning in whose name they pompously defy Catholic preachers and writers, saying to us: You speak of Christ and the Gospel—you cite them; but you are behind your age, Germany has now destroyed Christ and the Gospel; she has examined them by the light of criticism, and all that is nothing but a shadow, a dream, a myth!

Let us leave this triumph to pride; and with our sounder sense let us seek why the history of Jesus Christ lends itself to the attacks which I have just pointed out to you. Had Providence so willed it, Jesus Christ would have had but one single historian, conducting from one end to the other the thread of his life with a chronological clearness which would have given to each part its true place, and have raised the whole above any possible discussion. But Providence did not so will it. Providence desired that the Gospel should be the work of several men differing in age, in genius, in style, and in judgment, and not one of whom should collect under his pen all the materials of the life of Christ, but only simple fragments, the very choice of which was arbitrary. The idea of God in this was to make of the biography of his Son a miracle of intimate truth which the most vulgar eye might discern, and which was to be found in no other life of any man whatever. Indeed, from the first glance, the multiplicity of the Gospels is striking, not only from the title-page, which bears different names, but from the reflection of their personal nature in each of the Gospels. We see and feel that St. Matthew, St. Mark, St. Luke, St. John, are different souls, and that each traces in his own manner the likeness of his beloved Master, without taking the least account of what his neighbor is doing, or even of what the continuity of chronology requires. Thence an arbitrary choice of fragments, a default of connection, apparent contradictions, details omitted by one and related by another, a multitude of varieties of which men render no account to themselves. This is true. And yet in these four evangelists there is the same portraiture of Christ, the same sublimity, the same tenderness, the same force, the same language, the same accent, the same supreme singularity of physiognomy. Open St. Matthew, the publican, or St. John, the young man, chaste and contemplative; choose whatever passage you will in the one or in the other, different alike in matter and expression, and speak it before a thousand men assembled together, all will raise their heads; they recognize Jesus Christ. And the more the exterior disagreement of the Gospels is shown, the more that intimate agreement whence the moral unity of Christ springs will become a proof of their fidelity. If they unanimously represent so well the inimitable features of Christ, it is because he was before their eyes; they saw him such as he was and such as they were not able to forget him. They saw him with their senses, with their hearts, with the exactitude of a love which was to give its blood; they are at the same time witnesses, painters, and martyrs. That sitting of God before man has been witnessed only once, and this is why there is but one Gospel, although there were four evangelists.

And what soul is insensible to this? What soul will not one day forget science at the feet of Jesus Christ, represented by his apostles? To close this subject, listen to the words of a Frenchman, which will console you for the frenzies of that learning which the Gospel has not disarmed. They are those of a man whose judgment upon Jesus Christ I have already cited to you, and they express in clear and forcible language the impression which the reading of the Gospel leaves in the mind of the profane as well as in that of the Christian: "Shall we say that the Gospel history is a pure invention? My friend, men do not invent in this way, and the acts of Socrates, which no one doubts, are less fully proved than those of Jesus Christ. In truth, it is to push aside the difficulty without destroying it; it would be much more inconceivable that several men together should have fabricated that book than that only one should have furnished the subjects of it. The Jewish authors would never have acquired that tone or that morality; and the Gospel possesses characters of truth so great, so striking, so perfectly inimitable, that the inventor of it would be more marvellous than the hero!"

This is French language and French genius. And therefore you should not be surprised at returning to Christ after having quitted him The lucidity of our national intelligence sustains within you the light of grace, and causes you like giants to cross those thorny abysses of science, but of a science which braves the soul. Be faithful to this double gift which bears you towards God; judge of the power of Jesus Christ by the efforts, so contradictory and so vain, of his adversaries; and permit me to recall to you in terminating this discourse a celebrated trait which paints that power, and the eloquent prophecy which fifteen centuries have confirmed.

When the Emperor Julian attacked Christianity by that stratagem of war and violence which bears his name, and, absent from the empire, had gone to seek in battles the consecration of a power and popularity which he thought would achieve the ruin of Jesus Christ, one of his familiars, the rhetor Libanius, on meeting a Christian, asked him derisively and with all the insolence of assured success, what the Galilean was doing; the Christian answered: He is making a coffin. Some time afterwards Libanius pronounced the funeral oration of Julian over his mutilated body and his vanished power. What the Galilean was then doing, gentlemen, he does always, whatever may be the arm and the pride men may oppose to his cross. It would require much time to deduce all the famous examples of this; but we possess some which touch us closely, and by which Jesus Christ, at the extremity of ages, has confirmed to us the nothingness of his enemies. Thus, when Voltaire rubbed his hands with joy, towards the close of his life, saying to his followers: "In twenty years, God will see fine sport;" the Galilean prepared a coffin: it was that of the French monarchy. Thus, when a power of another order, but sprung, in some degree, from the same, held the Sovereign Pontiff in a captivity which threatened the fall at least of the temporal power of the vicar of Jesus Christ, the Galilean prepared a coffin: it was that of St. Helena. And now, on seeing Germany agitated by the convulsions of unregulated science, of which you have just witnessed so lamentable a production, we may say with as much certainty as hope: The Galilean prepares a coffin, and it is that of rationalism. And you all, sons of this age, ill-instructed by the miseries of past errors, and who seek out of Jesus Christ the way, the truth, and the life, the Galilean prepares a coffin for you; and it is that of all your most cherished conceptions. And so will it ever be, the Galilean ever working but two things, living of himself, or either by blood, oblivion, or shame, entombing all that is not of him.

THE EFFORTS OF RATIONALISM TO EXPLAIN THE LIFE OF JESUS CHRIST.

My Lord—Gentlemen,

Rationalism has then made but vain efforts to destroy and to pervert the life of Jesus Christ. Jesus Christ is not dethroned; the power of history protects and upholds him against all these attacks. Therefore rationalism has been forced to attempt a last and supreme effort to explain at least that life which it was unable either to destroy or to dishonor. We Catholics explain the life of Christ, we explain the success he has obtained—the greatest of all success, that of producing in minds the rational certainty of faith; in the soul, holiness by humility, chastity, and charity; in the world a spiritual community, one, universal, and perpetual—we explain it by that single expression: Jesus Christ is the Son of God. But if it be not so explained; if it be supposed that Christ is but a man, it is nevertheless necessary to give a reason for that greatest success ever obtained, which is his own. Now, as after the power of God there remains only the power of man, if Jesus Christ did not act by the power of God, he acted by the power of man. But the power of man in its results being manifestly inferior to that which Jesus Christ has accomplished, it follows that we must seek in man a certain root of power which, in rare cases, may suddenly appear and explain what Christ was and what he has accomplished. That is to say, that Jesus Christ, not being the Son of God, nor, as he himself said, the Son of man, he is the Son of mankind, the illustrious production of that silent and progressive action which is the life of mankind, and which, on certain solemn occasions, buds forth, so to say, blossoms, produces an extraordinary being, and surrounds him with a halo which all who come after him will confirm, up to the time when mankind, ever pregnant with the future, feels that it is imperfectly represented by the heroic and sovereign being it has produced, and at length salutes him with a last mark of respect, brings him down to the level of earthly things, and says to him: Adieu.

I shall devote our last conference of this year to the refutation of this system. This done, all that belongs to the constitution and character, alike of the Church and of Christ, having been manifested to you in our teaching, it will only remain for us to enter upon the doctrine itself of the Church and of Christ, in order to present it to you in all the fulness of its harmony; after which we shall have but to repose, you, gentlemen, from your attention, and I from the happiness of having taught you so long.

Three things have to be explained in the life and success of Jesus Christ: his doctrine which appears to surpass all others, the faith which the world has given to that doctrine, and, thirdly, the union of that doctrine and faith in a body hierarchically constituted, which is the Church. This triple phenomenon, it is said, is easily explained by the general state of doctrines, minds, and nations, at the time when Jesus Christ appeared. First, by the general state of doctrines. That of Jesus Christ is ordinarily considered to be a new doctrine, unknown, creative, as something which had neither root nor model in the past; this, as rationalism says, is a very palpable error. The human race has never been without doctrine; it is a necessary part of its life. That some simpleton satisfied in the debauch of pride and of the senses may pass through the world without troubling himself about doctrine, as a grain of dust carried along by the unstable wind passes and disappears, no one will deny. But mankind has other desires and other destinies. Mankind requires to know, to seek, to render account to itself of itself and of the universe, to possess a faith; and never, in reality, has it lived without that spiritual element. As men dig the earth that bears them, as they scan the sky that covers them, so they unceasingly labor upon the fertile soil of doctrines, in order to draw from them an aliment which they deem divine. This working is not less active in itself than that which is external and scientific, and they form together a tissue of unwearied action. Now there were three principal theatres of this action before Jesus Christ, the East, the West, and Judæa, which was the connecting link between the two others.

The East preserved doctrine under this form: that man had fallen, that he needed an expiation to return to a better condition—an expiation which, from cycle to cycle, favored mysterious incarnations of God. The eastern incarnation, its expiation, its metempsychosis or trial, nothing is more famous than these in the history of doctrines; and it will suffice to place these terms before your minds for you to perceive in a single moment, on penetrating to the heart of Judæa, this order of ideas still existing. In the West, a work of another nature had been accomplished. Under the reign of free discussion, it more effectually stripped itself of past myths; it sought wisdom, founded less upon tradition than upon the decisions of pure reason; and Plato was the most memorable instrument of these explorations of the human mind. He comprehended that God was in communication with man, not only by corrupted or lost traditions, but by the perpetual effusion of his Verb or Word within us, the Divine Word, the eternal *Logos*, absolute reason— of which our reason and our word are the transparent image, so that in contemplating his own ideas, man beheld, as in a mirror, the very ideas that are in God, and form there the first Word. And this theory of the manifestation of God by his Word, of which the word of man is but the diminutive and the reflection, had become the most elevated point of the doctrines of Greece and of the West. The Jewish people, on their part, had maintained, with extraordinary fidelity, the dogma of the unity of God, that of the creation,

12*

and in addition a certain hope of the fundamental unity of man, which should eventually be restored as it existed in the original family.

This was evidently the general state of doctrines at the time of Christ, and these doctrines, long isolated, each in its place, had at length met together after the conquests of Alexander and the invasions of Rome reaching to Asia. The East, the West, Judæa, and with them the Brahmins, the prophets, the sibyls, the sages, all the documents, and all the efforts of the past had, as it were, met together by common accord before the throne of Augustus, on the day when he closed upon the world the prophetic gates of the temple of war. At that moment Jesus Christ was born. Endowed with a genius answering to the marvellous circumstances of his age, he saw with a sure glance the confluence of doctrines; in that confluence he unravelled more than one fortuitous junction, he discovered there the germs of deeply-seated unity, and imagined that by giving satisfaction to all, by engrafting the East upon the West, the West and the East upon the Hebraic trunk, he should attain to a doctrine which would at least captivate a great multitude of minds in the divers parts of the world. He laid down as a foundation the eastern dogma of the fall, and declared that he himself, the last incarnation, superior to all that had preceded him, had come definitively to expiate the fault of the human race, and to restore to men with their native purity all their birthrights. Next, as the eastern incarnation was dishonored by too many fabulous elements, he based the idea of his own incarnation upon that Word of Plato, who had detached the communication between God and man from the traditional myth, in order to reduce it to a permanent communication of ideas in the very seat of the understanding. He declared that he was the Word of God, the reason of God, the one who, by his nature, enlightened every man coming into the world; and who, by the effective presence of his personality, by the exterior lights of his teaching, brought to the mind a more complete vision of truth. The Divine Word was thenceforth in presence of the human word; the image had but to look upon the model, the consequence had but to consult the principle, and from that confronting of within to without, of light to light, the supreme enlightenment of the human race would come. Plato thus became allied to the Brahmins of India, the West to the

East; and, in fine, to give satisfaction to the Hebraic ideas, Jesus Christ not only proclaimed himself the Messiah, he also accepted the dogmas of the unity of God and of the creation, which were inscribed in the first pages of the Bible, and which were the special patrimony of the Hebrew people.

Such was, gentlemen, according to rationalism, the theme of Jesus Christ, the mode of the formation of his doctrine, and the efficient cause of his doctrinal success. He was not creator, but electric; his success was not a success of creation, but of fusion. Before seeking to discover how far this is confirmed by comparing the Christian doctrines with the doctrines of antiquity, let us first see how Jesus Christ declared himself. Did he declare himself as a creator? Did he say: I am the inventor of truth? No, gentlemen, he said "I am the truth."[1] He said: "I am not come to destroy the law, but to fulfil it;"[2] which means: I am the truth of all times and places; I am that truth which was in the bosom of the Father; which appeared to the first man in the innocence of the terrestrial paradise; which the patriarchs, his successors, knew; which Noah on quitting

---

[1] St. John xiv. 6. [2] St. Matthew v. 17.

the ark received and promulgated afresh; which Abraham, in the fields of Chaldæa and Syria, saw and heard; which Moses, at the foot of Sinai, received, graven by the hand of God. I am that truth which is the first and the last, and which no man has ever been able totally to set aside. Behold, gentlemen, what Jesus Christ said of himself, and what the Church still says of him daily. He did not seek, nor do we seek for him a success of creation; we have never pretended that Christianity commenced with the appearance of Christ under Augustus. To have given it a character of novelty would have been to ruin Christianity. From the first day of the world, from the first word of God, from the first Divine ray which shone in our soul, it was Christ who acted, who spake, and who revealed himself; and that revelation spread over the whole earth with the dispersion of the primordial branches of the human race.

However, by the side of this phenomenon of the primitive and universal propagation of Christianity, we must remark that there grew up another of a very different character. I mean the progressive adulteration and corruption of Christianity by forgetfulness, reasoning, and unbelief.

So that Jesus Christ, although not new, brought into the world something which the world no longer knew save by ill-defined hopes and disfigured recollections. And, to begin by the East; it is true, the East had preserved the idea of the fall, of expiation, of the divine intervention for the restoration of man—no one will contest it; but the East had stifled that idea between two absurdities, namely, pantheism and metempsychosis; the one and the other affirming that the purification of man had for object and for effect the return of man to the very substance of the Divinity, from whence he had sprung, and that after cycles of trials, more or less prolonged, the final state of mankind would be that of the eternal and absolute repose of complete deification. Now, did Jesus Christ admit this doctrine? Did he compromise with the East in regard to pantheism or metempsychosis? No, he taught the very opposite; he said to us: You are but nothingness which has responded to the creating power of God; and your destiny, although great, is not to attain to God by confounding your substance with him, but by simple vision. You will one day see him, if you have believed in him; you will possess him present, if you have loved him absent; but your nature and your personality will subsist before him. Pantheism bears you alike too high and too low—too high in promising you that you are one in substance with God; too low in taking from you your proper nature and your principle of distinction. Your place and truth are not there. God and man are forever two; two in their essence; two in their personality; two in their love, for God made man from love; and if man correspond to that love which sought him the first, that same love will eternally reward him. If, on the contrary, man be unfaithful and ungrateful, that love will reject him eternally.

I ask you, gentlemen, was this the eastern dogma, or was it not rather its destruction?

And as to the West, they speak of Plato. But, in the first place, was Plato the whole West? Did he resume the West in himself? Did not Aristotle, Epicurus, Zeno, Pyrrho, exist by the same title, and did not their doctrines share with those of the Academy the empire of minds? You say that Plato was the highest expression of western wisdom; let us not contest it, and in seeing what he thought, let us see what Jesus Christ owed to him. In the metaphysical order,

Plato believed in the eternity of matter and of chaos, placing the world in presence of God as a substance inferior, but parallel and uncreated; in the moral order, he denied the existence of free-will, and affirmed in proper terms that no one was voluntarily bad, because the principle of all evil is an indeliberate error of the mind. Dualism and fatalism, such is that Plato so much admired—whom I have lauded myself, whom I shall still praise, a man admirable indeed, who, being plunged like all the others in the faint and almost extinguished light of antiquity, caught here and there glimpses of the shadow of truth, and made plaintive cries to it, as if he had beheld it; but being unable to seize it, had thrown again over his desires and his regrets that royal vestment which has become the charm of his thoughts, the beauty of his discourse, and the majesty of his renown. No sage ever equalled him in the invocation of truth, none foresaw its future more clearly, none ever tinged the twilight of error with a halo more gorgeous or better formed to solace the soul for wedding but a dream. But to make him an ancestor of Jesus Christ, and the tie by which the Gospel attached the West to itself, is to expect too much from his glory. Jesus Christ denied the Platonic dualism and fatalism, as he also denied the pantheism and metempsychosis of India; and if he called himself the Word, the Son of God, that expression sprang from a mystery which, to Plato, was unknown—the mystery of a triple personality in the substance, one and indivisible, of God.

The Jews, in their turn, although possessors of primitive Christianity and the expectation of the Messiah, had corrupted this deposit in their ideas, by making of Christian truth—which is the patrimony of all—their own special heritage, by substituting the idea of the law for the idea of faith. Moses for Christ, the personal for the universal. This is what St. Paul reproaches them with in the Epistle to the Romans, where he takes so much pains to explain to them the inferiority of the law to faith; how Christ was the principle of salvation from the time of Abraham, and how the works of the law, understood and performed without Jesus Christ, were a cause of death. The Jews rebelled against that forcible teaching; already steeped in the liberating blood, and even in communion with it, they persisted in venerating the idol which raised their national pride to the rank of a duty and a virtue, and persuaded themselves that Judaism was to subjugate the universe. In the Christian sense, this was true; in the sense in which they held it, it was false. Jesus Christ had then to combat Judæa as well as the East and the West. And if you would see yet more clearly that Christian doctrine was not a success of fusion, but a success of contradiction—of contradiction to the East, to the West, to the Hebrew people—you have but to study pantheism as the East has preserved it, Judaism as the remnant of Israel still understands it, and Platonism as it has been resuscitated before our eyes.

Pantheism lives in India. India is now, as in past times, its land of predilection, it lives there under the same forms and in the same doctrines as in the time of Jesus Christ. Now, no country, no system, has offered more resistance to the Christian apostolate. For three centuries the great Indian peninsula has been open to us; many European nations have together and successively governed it. England is now its mistress; we hold it by our missionaries as by our arms under the grasp of our domination, and nowhere, not even in that China which is closed to us, has the action of Jesus Christ been less rewarded with success. Brahminism has resisted

example as well as discussion; it has been like
granite against truth, like a thing incompatible
with another thing, and which rejects it so much
the more as it approaches nearer. Many reasons
have been given for this, such as the rule of caste,
and the aversion resulting therefrom for our principles of equality. It may be also that on account
of the many traditions it has preserved on the fall
and reparation, Brahminism has been less sensible
to the mystery of redemption by the blood of
Jesus Christ, as we see men in whom the possession of a certain measure of truth serves as an ob-
stacle to the acquisition of the rest. The honest
man is often in this state, gentlemen, when he has
the misfortune not to be a Christian; his probity
keeps him from God, whilst the unworthy sinner,
looking upon himself, sees nothing within that
raises an illusion for him. This is why Jesus
Christ said: "Those women whom you call lost
will go into the kingdom of heaven before you." [1]
They are, in fact, nearer to good by being far from
it; they touch the feet of Jesus Christ by humil-
iation; and when we are at the feet of Jesus
Christ we are very near to his heart. So perhaps
is it with nations that have lost all truth; they

---

[1] St. Matt. xxi. 31.

feel the need of regaining it, whilst those who still preserve vestiges of truth, grow proud with the little they have, scorning to desire and seek that which they have not. Be that as it may, Indian pantheism has not changed; it is now what it was in the Augustan age; and whatever may have been the cause of its insensibility towards Jesus Christ, it no less proves to us how chimerical is the idea of that fusion of doctrines by which it is desired to explain the formation of the Christian dogma.

The spectacle of Judaism as it lives before us leads us to the same conclusion. And as to Platonism, God has permitted it to resuscitate in our time, so that on witnessing it in action we may be able to judge of its doctrinal sympathy for Jesus Christ. You all know to what school I allude; you know how that school has restored Platonic dualism to honor, by rejecting from its philosophy the fundamental dogma of the creation of the world by God, and you know also how it treats the rest of Christianity. In contemporary literature we have no more avowed enemies than the friends of Plato. Whether then we regard pantheism, Judaism, or Platonism—all three subsisting before us as in the time of Jesus Christ—it is easy for us to judge that Christianity was not the result of a fusion between the doctrines of the ancient world, but a work of renovation and of contradiction. The Gospel has renewed all, because all had been forgotten; it has contradicted all, because all had been denied or disfigured; it has had all doctrines for adversaries, because it has disavowed and rejected all. And as it was aforetime, so it is now. The dogmatic intolerance of which it is accused defines its nature and proves its originality.

But the success of Jesus Christ was not only realized in the powerful and aboriginal formation of his doctrine; it was also a success of faith. A doctrine is as nothing as long as it has not taken possession of minds by faith, which gives it life and action. How did the ancient world believe in Jesus Christ? How did the men of the East and the West, the learned or the unlearned, and, in fine, the great nations, abdicate the teaching they had received from the past, in order to become the disciples of a Jew crucified in Jerusalem? Rationalism explains it thus: At the epoch of Augustus the human mind was weary. On the one hand, it no longer accepted idolatry, which was the popular form of ancient doctrines: and on the other, philosophy having founded nothing, a double lassitude of the intelligence ensued—lassitude as to public religion, and lassitude as to the powerless efforts of philosophy. Men wandered in the void and at hazard, invoking a new faith. Jesus Christ came; he inaugurated before the world, fatigued and ready to receive it, an affirmation which did but slight violence to general opinion; he was listened to, men wanted to believe, and they believed in him.

For my part, gentlemen, I have no belief in this genesis of the Christian faith. When an epoch has lost faith it is not so easy to give it back again, and we have some proof of this before our eyes. Rationalism, in such times, invades all hearts, and rationalism is never convinced of its impotency, or weary of itself. If four or five centuries of useless efforts before Jesus Christ had discouraged it, it should now, when it counts eighteen centuries more of vain endeavors, be on the eve of abdicating its pretensions. Does it, I ask you, even dream of so doing? Do we not see it more affirmative, more arrogant, more sure of itself than ever? So will it be a thousand years hence. A thousand years hence our posterity will see masters who will ascend the rostrum and say to them with imperturbable self-possession: Gentlemen, we are about to create philosophy, or at least, if we have not that honor, we touch the fortunate epoch which will place the crowning stone upon its edifice. Such is rationalism. No experience has wearied or will ever weary it of itself; it rises anew from its ashes, or rather, it neither lives nor dies, but is a credulous infant who aspires to maturity without ever once leaving its cradle. Let us not wonder thereat; it takes its starting-point in a principle which excludes life, because it excludes faith; and yet faith will destroy it. It has but the choice of death; and it naturally prefers that which leaves to it the appearance of being something, were it but a doubt and a negation. Rationalism is incorrigible because to correct itself it must cease to exist.

To admit then that the general state of minds, in the Augustan age, was a state of void and lassitude, is by no means to explain the propagation of the Christian faith then accomplished with so much power and rapidity. But I do not admit that such was, under Augustus, the general state of minds. Doubtless idolatry had become an object of contempt to a great number of enlightened men, but the people did not despise it. The popular mind sympathized with idolatry, which more than ever included all the recollections which the multitude adored and all the spectacles they needed. The political spirit favored that tendency; it supported idolatry as a State necessity. And when Jesus Christ came to ask from Rome that right of citizenship which she had refused to none of the gods she had vanquished, it was easy to see what was the state of the popular and political spirit upon this head. Do we not know what answer she gave to him? Do we not know who replied to the martyrs of Christ, in the amphitheatres, by insults and cries of death? Whilst the emperors and the proconsuls gave sentence against them in the name of the political spirit, the people issued theirs also in the form and power peculiar to them. The empire shed the blood, the people called for it; and, after having obtained it, they threw it at the face of Christ. And, behind the empire and the people, rationalism, forming the rear-guard of idolatry, eagerly fed its pen from the sources of error. Those Platonists, so puffed up with their spiritualism, were seen tearing up the Gospel page by page, perverting its meaning, and launching forth their maledictions against it; they were seen parading their affection for Jupiter and all the old gods, writing genealogies for them, consecrating a new philosophy, bearing offerings to them; nothing was left untried, neither science, nor sarcasm, nor energy, nothing that could be turned into an outrage or an argument against Christianity. Is this what they call the lassitude of minds? Is this the tacit conjuration of the times in favor of Christ? Ah! when at length he had won the faith of the world, and when the successors of his apostles appeared at Nicea, their mutilated visages showed whether they came from peace or war, whether they had been favored or persecuted, whether the popular spirit, the political spirit, the rationalist spirit, had or had not been their servitors, and what was the real value of those systems invented after the fact, by which the life of the patient is explained by the tyrant who caused his death. Julian, at least, said what was true: "Galilean, thou hast conquered!"

Here we find again, in regard to the formation of the Christian dogma, not the principle of fusion, but the principle of contradiction. Jesus Christ contradicted all minds as he contradicted all doctrines, he conquered all minds as he conquered all doctrines: such is the truth.

It was not, however, enough for him to found a doctrine and obtain faith; it was not enough to found a doctrine in contradicting all other doctrines, to found a spirit of faith in contradicting every other spirit. He had in addition to found a Church, that is to say, a society of men living by that doctrine and faith. Rationalism, in order to explain his success, invokes here the general state of nations. It says that in the time of Augustus a double want was felt, namely, a want of liberty and unity. The nations one after another had borne the yoke of the Romans; and, stripped of their independence, victims of the increasing rapacity of the proconsuls, they marked the progress of Roman corruption, watching, like all who were in bondage, for that hour of weakness which inevitably follows prosperity when it is without limit or counterpoise. That hour advanced rapidly; Jesus Christ came also, at the same time, at the precise moment. And what brought he? The elevation of the lowly, in the idea of a common origin and a holy brotherhood; strength to the weak, to women, to children, in the idea of a new domestic right; help to oppressed peoples, in the idea of a universal republic founded by God himself and governed by him. What could be more attractive, more sure of success? When then Jesus Christ appeared, and when from the heart of Judæa the very air had borne even to the ends of the world his emancipating word, with what a thrill of sacred hope must the world have stood up and watched! What wonder if women, children, those who toiled, the slaves, the poor, the despised of every kind and of every country, went forth to meet him, cast their garments under his feet, cut down branches from the trees and strewed them in his way, not once only, when he entered into Jerusalem on the eve of his death, but even after his death, unwilling to believe he was dead, and crying to his disciples as to him: "Hosanna to the Son of David! Blessed is he that cometh in the name of the Lord."[1] That hosanna was the cry of deliverance, the response to him who had heard the groanings of men; and from wheresoever he came, whatsoever name he took, whatsoever his race or his design, man or God, it was impossible for him not to be accepted as he presented himself. What it matters to the prisoner,

---

[1] St. Matt. xxi. 9.

set free, whence liberty comes to him? To the miserable, to the oppressed, whence the deliverer comes?

"Who saves his country is inspired from heaven!"

I grant, gentlemen, that these ideas are full of charm; it touches us to think that when nations are slaves and corrupted, they aspire to their emancipation. But, alas! history pronounces another judgment than the heart of man. We learn from history that nations fallen into servitude do not desire liberty. As the apostate from truth inveighs against truth, so the apostate from liberty, the nation which has lost it by its fault— and it is always lost by its own fault, by taking the heart of a slave—that nation no longer aspires to regain it. It suffers, it is degraded; but to feel its misfortune and to reconquer the treasure it has lost requires the heart of the free man; that heart it has no longer. It loves the wages of servitude, and dreads the duties of liberty, especially of that which it has lost, and which is to be purchased at such a price. It would have to despise even its very life, to be ready to throw it to the winds, so that some slight lesson might be learned from its death, and that its last sigh, even remotely, might serve to bring about deliverance and honor. The enslaved nation knows not this heroism, and perhaps despises it. You have proofs of this, gentlemen, elsewhere even than in history; and passing over the continent of Europe, I will take you at once to the shores of Africa. Observe the negro there. You send your squadrons to protect his liberty against the conspiracy of the slave-dealer; doubtless you do well; it is perhaps a duty, it is certainly an honor. But are you simple enough to believe that you will prevent this traffic? Wherever man wills to sell himself, he finds buyers; wherever hearts of slaves meet together, they form masters, even when they do not find them already prepared. As long as the negro will sell the flesh and blood of his countryman, all the squadrons of the civilized world will not lift him from the consequences of that horrible baseness of heart; and it is the same, more or less, with all nations bent under the yoke of servitude and corruption. They seek no deliverance, but the price only of their soul and body; and they are sufficiently recompensed for the abjection of slavery by the abjection of vice. This was the state of the Roman world. Jesus Christ, it is true, brought them liberty, but with virtue and by virtue. The cost was too great for them; they

…id not accept it. Even after the Church was founded, the empire continued in decadency; it fell from Diocletian to the eunuchs of Constantinople; and when the West, renewed by the barbarians, willed to go to its help, even to the very centre of the East, when it armed all its chivalry to save it, that wretched people extended to the Latin hand only a hand incapable of sincerity. They treasonably rejected the blood given to it, fearing the too near approach of men who knew how to wield the sword and to devote themselves.

Jesus Christ may well found a Church, but not regenerate an empire. He formed free souls in forming pious souls, whom he drew to himself from the midst of the general corruption; but the nations did not answer to his call, as nations, in order to manifest that his work was not the result of political circumstances in which the course of things had led mankind. He had against him the passion of servitude, instead of having in his favor the want of emancipation. And such is still the state of his Church here below. Although favorable to all the legitimate rights which together form the honor and liberty of nations, she unceasingly raises up against herself the instincts of servitude, under the very name of liberty. They ask license from her, and propose to her oppression: it is the cry of nature in all times. In refusing both of these, now as heretofore, she doubtless responds to the real wants of mankind; but she responds to them after the manner of God, by a force which imposes itself and by a blessing whose glory none but the benefactor can claim.

It is the same in regard to unity. I do not deny that the Roman empire, by subjecting many diverse peoples under a common administration, had spread in minds the idea of a vast social organization. But that idea, in the degree in which it existed, did not pass over the very limited circle of a purely political domination. They did not perceive, even in the depths of that unity, the idea that the human race was a single being or a single body. By unity, they understood that one single nation became master of the others; one Cæsar, the Cæsar of the world; but of the spiritual unity of souls by faith, hope, and charity, under a single visible chief, the representative and vicar of God, they had not even the most confused notion. As soon as the universal Church had advanced a step in the world, and had thus revealed this secret of her destiny, it gave rise only to an immense fear, the enduring repercussion of which she still feels. The passion of nationality is as strong now against the Church as it was eighteen centuries ago; and those even who aspire to the social unity of the human race cannot endure the idea of the Christian republic, other than as a figure or a pattern which they use to represent their own conception. What philosopher or what statesman dreams of unity in the Christian sense, save to fear and detest it? You see, gentlemen, that in examining facts, not only ancient but present, we arrive at the same conclusion, namely, that the principle of the success of Jesus Christ, whether in regard to the formation of his doctrine, or to the propagation of his faith or the establishment of his Church, was not a principle of fusion, but a principle of contradiction. As he had contradicted all doctrines by his own, all minds by his own, he has contradicted all nations by his Church, that is to say, he has braved and still braves, in the perpetuity of his work, all the combined forces of mankind.

Let us go further, gentlemen, and seek the supreme cause of that contradiction. Let us seek why Jesus Christ contradicts all and is contradicted by all—too often even by those who possess his faith, who belong to his Church, who eat his flesh and drink his blood. The cause of this is not in the region of the mind; rationalism deceives itself in seeking there the explanation of the Christian mystery. Jesus Christ advances beyond the intelligence, he reaches even the soul, which is the centre of all, and demands from it the sacrifice of its most cherished inclinations, in order to convert it from evil to good, from pride to humility, from sensuality to chastity, from enjoyment to mortification, from egotism to charity, from corruption to holiness. And man opposes thereto an obstinate resistance; he arms against Jesus Christ his reason, his heart, the world, the human race, heaven and earth; and even when vanquished by the sense of his misery and by the tested gentleness of the yoke of the Gospel, he does not cease to feel within himself, even to his last moment, a possibility and a secret desire to revolt. Here the whole secret lies. And if you would understand how difficult is the triumph of Jesus Christ, I propose to you, not the conversion of the world, but of one single man. I ask you, princes of nations, you who command by intelligence, wealth, or power, I ask you to make a man humble and chaste, a penitent, a soul who judges his pride and his senses, who despises himself, who hates himself, who struggles against himself, and either as proof or as the means of his conversion, humbly avows the errors of his life. I ask but this from you. Can you accomplish it? Have you ever done so? Ah! if a king, radiant in the majesty of the throne, were to call you into his cabinet, and press you to confess your faults at his feet, you would say to him: Sire, I would rather confess them to the man who makes shoes for my feet! If the most famous philosopher of his age were to use all his eloquence to persuade you to kneel and confess your sins to him, you would not deign even to turn away from laughing in his face. Pardon these expressions, gentlemen, they would be ill-placed on other occasions; here, they are but just and grave. And yet, what kings, philosophers, and nations are unable to obtain, a poor priest, a man unknown, the most obscure among men, daily accomplishes in the name of Jesus Christ. He sees souls touched by their misery, coming to seek him who knows them not, and avow to him in all sincerity the degradations of their passions. It is the door by which men enter into Jesus Christ, by which they repose in him, by which the

Church herself enters; for the Church is but the world penitent; and that single word reveals to you the whole miracle of her foundation and perpetuity, as it will also explain to you the force of active and passive contradiction which is in Jesus Christ. Jesus Christ contradicts all doctrines, because his doctrine is holy and the world is corrupt; he contradicts every spirit, because his spirit is holy and the world is corrupt; he contradicts all nations, because his Church is holy and the world is corrupt; and for the same reason the world contradicts the doctrines, the spirit, and the Church of Jesus Christ.

It was then with justice, in a certain sense, that in the first proceedings directed against Christians, by the orders of Nero, they were convicted, according to Tacitus, of "hatred against the human race." They hated, in fact, all that the world esteemed; they pursued all its ideas and all its affections, in order to destroy them utterly; and although they did this from love for the world, the world was not bound to understand and thank them for it. Even charity, so new was it, clothed herself in hostile colors, and the death of Jesus Christ upon the cross—that masterpiece of love—appeared rather like an insult than devotedness. All was contradiction, because all was God; and in order to prove that nothing of this was of man, Jesus Christ was for ever to be recognized by this sign, according as it was said of him at the moment of his first appearing among men: "This child is set up for a sign which shall be contradicted."[1] And he himself, recalling the prophecies, said to his enemies: "The stone which the builders rejected has become the corner-stone; the Lord hath done this, and it is wonderful in our eyes."[2] The prophecy is still accomplished daily; princes, nations, savants, sages, the skilful, the builders, in fine, reject the stone; they declare it to be unfit or worn out by time; they will accept it no longer; and yet it is still "the corner-stone, and it is wonderful in our eyes." It supports all, although it is rejected by all; it possesses the double character of necessity and impossibility. Recognize here, gentlemen, a struggle between two unequal wills—the will of man which revolts, and the will of God which causes itself to be obeyed by man, in man, and in spite of man. And you Christians, sons of this work wherein God gives you so favored a place, learn the need of constant suffering, of not triumphing

---

[1] St. Luke ii. 34. [2] St. Matt. xxi. 42.

by triumph, that Jesus Christ may not be accused of owing something to man, but of triumphing upon the cross, so that your victory may be of God, and that you may be able, now and henceforth, to repeat those words which, after so many other signs witnessed by you, express the highest sign of the divinity of Jesus Christ: "The stone which the builders rejected has become the cornerstone; the Lord hath done this, and it is wonderful in our eyes!"

THE END.

P. O'SHEA'S
New Publications,
AND
NEW EDITIONS OF IMPORTANT BOOKS.

LACORDAIRE'S WORKS.

LACORDAIRE'S CONFERENCES ON GOD.
One vol. royal 8vo, cloth, bevelled......................$3.00

LACORDAIRE'S CONFERENCES ON OUR LORD JESUS CHRIST.
One vol. royal 8vo, cloth................................$3.00

LACORDAIRE'S CONFERENCES ON THE CHURCH.
One vol. royal 8vo......................................$5.00

LIVES OF THE DECEASED BISHOPS OF THE CATHOLIC CHURCH IN THE UNITED STATES.
By Richard H. Clarke, A.M. Two vols. imperial 8vo, superbly printed, bound, and illustrated..........................$8.00

GENERAL HISTORY OF THE CHURCH.
By Darras. With an Introduction and Notes by Archbishop Spalding. Four vols. 8vo, cloth......................$12.00

SERMONS FOR THE TIMES.
By Rev. D. A. Merrick, S.J. One vol. 12mo, elegantly printed and bound...$1.50

LECTURES ON THE CHURCH.
By Rev. D. A. Merrick, S.J. One vol. 12mo............$1.50

RULES FOR THE CHOICE OF A STATE OF LIFE.
By Rev. R. F. Aug. Damanet, S.J. Cloth................ 30

MANUAL OF THE HOLY NAME OF JESUS.

An elegant Prayer-Book, specially recommended to young men. By the DOMINICAN FATHERS. Flexible morocco............ $1.00

THE AGNUS DEI: ITS HISTORY AND USE.

By a FATHER OF THE SOCIETY OF JESUS. Flexible cloth.... 20

THE CROWN OF MARY; OR, THE ROSARY.

With Illustrations and Meditations. By a DOMINICAN FATHER. 18mo, paper... 10

THE KNOWLEDGE AND LOVE OF JESUS CHRIST.

By Rev. FATHER SAINT JURE, S.J. Three vols., cloth, bevelled... $7.50

THE SPIRIT OF SAINT FRANCIS OF SALES.

One vol. 12mo, cloth, bevelled.......................... $2.00

MEDITATIONS FOR EVERY DAY IN THE YEAR.

By Rev. FATHER CRASSET, S.J......................... $1.80

TREATISE ON THE LOVE OF GOD.

By SAINT FRANCIS DE SALES. One vol. 12mo............ $1.75

INTRODUCTION TO A DEVOUT LIFE.

By SAINT FRANCIS OF SALES. 18mo..................... 75

INSTRUCTIONS ON THE COMMANDMENTS AND SACRAMENTS.

By St. LIGUORI. 32mo................................. 40

THE CATHOLIC YOUTH'S HYMN-BOOK.

The best collection of Catholic Hymns extant, with music, &c., &c. Compiled by the BROTHERS OF THE CHRISTIAN SCHOOLS, with a special view to the WANTS of CATHOLIC SCHOOLS. 4to...... 60

———— Cheap edition, *without music*................... 15

THE ILLUSTRATED PROGRESSIVE SERIES OF READING AND SPELLING BOOKS.

THE BEST SERIES PUBLISHED.

P. O'SHEA, Publisher,

27 Barclay Street, New York.

www.ingramcontent.com/pod-product-compliance
Lightning Source LLC
Chambersburg PA
CBHW022110230426
43672CB00008B/1327